FACING

CO-AKK-452

FACING HISTORY AND OURSELVES

37921

c2

Facing History and Ourselves
Christian Brothers University
Kenrick Hall
650 E. Parkway S., Memphis, TN 38104-5581

IN THE EYE OF THE STORM

I tried to impress upon them that "Jewish eyes are constantly filled with fear. Otherwise, Jews don't look different from Poles or Ukrainians. There is no particular smell in your body that will betray you. It is that eternal terror in your eyes that marks you. Get rid of it!"

IN THE EYE
OF THE
STORM:
A MEMOIR OF SURVIVAL
THROUGH THE HOLOCAUST

BY
Uri Lichter

Preface by (Rev.) Theodore M. Hesburgh, C.S.C.

INTRODUCTION BY EUGENE DAVIDSON

HOLOCAUST LIBRARY
New York, NY 10011

Copyright © 1987, by Ire (Uri) Lichter

All rights reserved,
including the right to reproduce
this book or parts thereof in any form.

For information address:
THE BROOKDALE PRESS
184 Brookdale Road
Stamford, Connecticut 06903

ISBN: 0-89604-088-7 (Holocaust Library)

Library of Congress Catalog Number: 87-80771

LIBRARY OF CONGRESS CATALOGING IN PUBLICATION DATA
Lichter, Uri.
In the eye of the storm.

1. Lichter, Uri. 2. Jews—Ukraine—L'vov—Biography.
3. Holocaust, Jewish (1939–1945)—Ukraine—L'vov—
Personal narratives. 4. L'vov (Ukraine)—Biography.
I. Title.
DS135.R95L455   1987   947'.718   87–80771
ISBN 0-89604-088-7

Manufactured in The United States of America
by RAY FREIMAN & COMPANY
Stamford, Connecticut 06903

*I dedicate this book
to my dear wife, Fenia,
and my two sons, William and Nathan,
their wives and children,
to my father who survived with us
and passed away in 1965,
those members of my family
who did not survive,
especially my mother
and my older sister Riwka.
My deep thanks also,
to that truly "Righteous Polish" family,
the Prachtels.*

ACKNOWLEDGEMENTS

MY GREATEST SUPPORT came from my wife, Fenia. She was the first person to listen to my odyssey. Our sons, William and Nathan, urged me to write and helped me to expand my rough notes. Re-reading my handwritten draft was a difficult experience, bringing back nightmares and causing sleepless nights. The manuscript was first type-written by Nathan, after which William helped me put the story into narrative form.

The process was not complete until I met Frank Stiffel. One of the rare survivors of Lvov, Treblinka and Auschwitz, he is also a writer. He helped me to fill out the story and provided the first editing.

With the help of these and other family members and friends, I am now able to present the story of my fight for survival in the eye of the storm.

₩ ₩ ₩ ₩ ₩ ₩

PREFACE

It is always the little people—the *anawim*—who suffer most from the ambitions of the powerful. The wars unleashed by their ambitions sweep families and homesteads like so much flotsam, in their wake. For the little people have no protection but their own ingenuity. Now and again, however, that native ingenuity coupled with a keen instinct for survival allows a family to emerge—seldom intact it seems, yet a family nonetheless. For, it is families and homesteads which shape our societies and only families can root again after the surface of their land has been devastated. What is even more miraculous however, is to hear their tale, for little people are taught not to raise their voices and thus are seldom heard. So this story offers us a twin miracle: passage to life and the story of that passage to embolden our hearts.

This passage is more than survival however, as the Nazi devastation was worse than pillage. Fueled by a neo-pagan ideology and abetted by pervasive Christian distrust of Jews, the special target of this destructive force was the people whom God had chosen as His own. An anachronism to Christians and an affront to enlightenment Europe, Jews became a convenient and highly visible scapegoat for the frustrations of a fearful Nazi leadership.

The ritual of loading the community's sins on a hapless goat each year on the Day of Atonement, was spelled out in the book of Leviticus and the pattern is as extensive as humanity itself. For a scapegoat must always be found to deflect the violence which unrestrained ambition brings in its wake. Yet violence so deflected is not quenched—only momentarily appeased. In fact, the violent sacrifice of a ritual victim only feeds more violence.

And so it was at Auschwitz and a score of other efficient ovens, in eastern Europe during the rise and precipitious decline of the Thousand Year Reich. Will the voices of the little people—the *anawim*—rising out of that calculated yet wanton destruction, embolden us to confront the roots of violence in ourselves and in the societies of which we are a part? *That* is the poignant question this account presses upon us. Ingenuity alone will not suffice, for it can be put at the service of extermination as well as survival. Gratitude will help, but, above all, wonder and awe: at the story of this family's resurrection to life and the call of that story to put our lives to the service of reconciliation, in a world still fueled by violence.

(Rev.) Theodore M. Hesburgh, C.S.C.
President, University of Notre Dame

‖‖ ‖‖ ‖‖ ‖‖ ‖‖ ‖‖

INTRODUCTION

The author of this extraordinary book survived the years of the second World War in one of the world's epicenters of anti-Semitism. It was a borderland country where Poles, Ukranians and Germans might make and break short-term political alliances, but where anti-Semitism was endemic and seemingly forever. In times of peace the Christian populations of whatever nationality were likely to avoid contact with Jews except for practical purposes like trade; after the war started, they watched the deportations impassively and in many cases helped the Nazi authorities seek out Jews. Anti-Semitism was one of the few things these people had in common and the narrator, Uri Lichter, could not have found himself in a more unlikely place for the survival of himself and those members of his family he would be able to rescue.

How he made his way in this enemy country in the midst of which he and his family lived and where his mother, an older sister and nearly all of his co-religionists perished is told in these pages. Although the story is mainly one of unrelenting hostility there are notable exceptions; like the Polish mother and daughter named Prachtel, who at the risk of their own lives sheltered the author's younger sister during the entire war. The Prachtel father, a Polish judge, had himself been deported in 1939 and was never heard from again. But despite her own troubles his wife did not hesitate to take the ten year old Jewish girl into her family, where the child remained in safety until the end of the war.

Lichter's story is a tale of survival against all odds, survival achieved with guile, with forged documents that transformed the Lichter father and brothers into Poles and or Volksdeutsche enabling the brothers to work with and on the enemy. The family's deeply held religious convictions were both an invisible armor and a constant threat to reveal who they really were. Even their daily bread, when they could get it, presented a moral problem; the sons were forced to eat forbidden food which the father steadfastly refused to do. This was the only way they could maintain the physical strength they needed, to keep their emaciated father alive.

Their ordeal transformed them from everyday, honest trades-people into indomitable resisters. They had no resources beyond themselves and the occasional help of some people they encountered, none of whom, probably, knew they were Jews.

Since the author is writing only of what he and his family experienced, his narrative can have no place for recording the facts of allies unknown to them, in unlikely places and positions; like the Prussian General Johannes Blaskowitz who commanded an army in Poland. Blaskowitz had risked and won the Fuhrer's disfavor by protesting the atrocious actions of the SS Einsatz Groups, as they operated against the Jews in Poland. He wrote that the troops regarded the SS and police with something "between abhorrence and hate. Every solider," he writes, "finds himself sickened and revolted by these crimes committed by members of the Reich and representa-tives of the power of the state. We do not understand how such things, especially since they occur so to speak, under our protection, can possibly go unpunished."

Or for scenes like that in a courtroom in Jerusalem, years later, where the spectators at a session of the Eichman trial, spontaneously rose to their feet to honor a witness. He was the Lutheran Dean, Heinrich Grueber, himself a survivor of two concentration camps, who had been responsible for the survival of some of the 1500 Jews harbored during the war by Berliners, many of whom had never before laid eyes on the hunted individuals they helped save.

What the author does tell us is, on the face of it, true; the substance of his story is corroborated by scores of other eye-witness accounts and it is as dramatic as any television cliff-hanger. This is the way he remembers what went on and this, we accept, is the way it really was.

The story has its ironic episodes. Lichter at one point was provided with a chauffer while he worked for a Nazi owned construc-tion firm in occupied Russian territory. There he carried out the job of a skilled engineer for which he had no previous training, while he managed to sabotage his own work. It was a chancy time, in which he could one day thrive as a pseudo-member of the Master Race and the next be one of its victims, on a freight train on his way to execution.

As the National Socialist state was going down in flames and ashes the author celebrated his deliverance by the Red army. It was a world-shaking victory and it would be pleasant to report that it took with it the last vestiges of the infamous fable of the *Protocols of Zion*.

But such was not to be, and willing hands picked up embers of the torch Hitler had dropped. Some two years after the Lichters arrived in the United States, Joseph Stalin imagined a deadly conspiracy of Jewish doctors and a new purge was in the making when he died.

Stalin's successors have found other means of demonstrating their displeasure with Jews and although undoubtedly motivated more by political than religious or ethnic considerations, ranged the Soviet Union with the coalition that seeks the destruction of the State of Israel. Arab countries and developing nations have called for a Jihad, holy war, against the Jewish state and even accused *it* of genocide; anti-Semitic terrorists have plied their trade, as have white and black exhorters on behalf of anti-Semitic and racial causes in the United States. Austrians, once over-represented in the SS, with due deliberation chose as their President, in 1986, a man who had concealed his Nazi past, until it was revealed by others during his campaign.

Clearly the story Uri Lichter tells will remain a cautionary tale.

Eugene Davidson

Eugene Davidson, author and editor, long an associate at Yale University Press as editor and Chairman of the Publications Committee, has recently been named Honorary President of the Conference on European Problems. He is the author of THE DEATH AND LIFE OF GERMANY; THE TRIAL OF THE GERMANS; THE NUREMBERG FALLACY; THE MAKING OF ADOLF HITLER and is now completing work on a new book dealing with Hitler's last years.

Author's FOREWORD

THIS IS A MEMOIR of my fight for survival. It is also the story of my family's struggle with fate, as the Jews of Europe, of Poland, and particularly of the city of Lvov were being murdered by the Nazis and their collaborators.

The events described in this book occurred in the years 1941–1944. The places stretch from Lvov to the southwestern Ukraine. My family and I lived under assumed identities, hoping, simply to live long enough to see sanity return to the world. I kept my notes, letters, and various other documents so that one day I would be able to publish the facts about the ugliness of those days.

Writing the story had to wait until now, however, because my fight to survive continued after the war. My immediate priorities then were my responsibility to my family, and adaptation to my new country, the United States. I arrived here in 1951 and first had to learn a new language and a radically different way of life. I was fortunate. Although its streets aren't paved with gold, America is a wonderful country and Miami, Florida a beautiful place in which to live. I was surrounded by freedom of opportunity, and with hard work I benefited from what I found.

Uri Lichter

‖‖ ‖‖ ‖‖ ‖‖ ‖‖ ‖‖

CONTENTS

PROLOGUE

ON OCTOBER 10, 1943, toward the end of the Jewish
Day of Atonement, four figures gathered secretly in the
back room of a peasant cottage in Dolginzewo, a little
industrial town about a hundred kilometers south of Dnepropetrovsk in south western Soviet Ukraine — a land
which, for two years, had been in the grip of Hitler's armed
forces and Political Security Police. The Ukraine swarmed
with regular Wehrmacht soldiers, the Waffen SS, the uniformed and plain clothes Gestapo and innumerable
Ukrainian collaborators.

The four were a father and his three young sons who
were employees of the railroad construction company from
Germany, L. Wening Bauunternehmung, Dolginzewo.

They had congregated for no less a purpose than to utter the Neilah, the Prayer of Conclusion, which is normally recited before the shofar, or ram's horn, announces that one more Yom Kippur, Day of Atonement, has come to an end. In this prayer a Jew accepts God's verdict of death or life in the year to come. For these four, another year of horror and uncertainty was about to begin.

The oldest of the group had documents that made him out to be sixty-five years of age, old enough to be called starik, old man, in Russian. He was actually fifty five, but an older man was thought to be somewhat safer from being sent to work camp. He was clean-shaven except for a thin mustache, five feet four inches tall, and had a lean face and an emaciated body, all of which suggested a latter-day Don Quixote in appearance. His name was Wladyslaw Tyszkiewicz, or so the documents read.

The youngest was a skinny, blond, thirteen-year-old, called by his documents, Stasio Grabowski. His personality had not yet stabilized. He could swing from macho one day to saint on another. The third, also a teenager, with tousled brown hair looked older. His documents stated that Piotr Siminski was seventeen years old. The last was dark blond, blue-eyed, with a short clipped mustache — Stanislaw Nowak age twenty-four.

Nowak was the originator, moving force and buttress of this fragile cell of modern Marranos — Jews pretending to be not only Poles, but sometimes Volksdeutsche, ethnic Germans of Polish citizenship.

In normal times, a minyan, or quorum of ten males older than thirteen years of age, is required for prayers to be acceptable to the God of Israel. But times were not normal, and the doctrine of Pekuach Nefesh prevailed. The Jewish sages taught that man is the apex of God's creation, the highest level in the order of value, and that since life is God's greatest good, man is obliged to cherish and preserve it. The rabbis ruled that the obligation to preserve life supersedes all other commandments; thus, in dire circumstances, an orthodox Jew may eat non-kosher food, work on the Sabbath, and be excused from the fast on Yom Kippur, and, of course, under certain circumstances, a minyan may be excused.

These four men, however, had with them a huge company of shadows, the souls of Jews who had been murdered in the last few years. In such a congregation they whispered prayers, made their confessions of sins and vowed to become better in the year to come. Their prayers mingled mourning, despair and hope.

The old man finished by saying the Kaddish, the mourners' prayer, for their loved ones and for the entire Jewish community. Then they sat and waited for the first star to appear — God's messenger of the end and the beginning.

At one point, the starik rose and slipped cautiously out to the little orchard behind the house. After a short absence, he returned noiselessly, his taut face aglow with spiritual joy, and he whispered in Yiddish: "Kinderlach! Mir kennen schoyn essen. Children! We may now eat."

His words replaced the penetrating sound of the shofar. Yom Kippur for the year 1943 in the Christian Era had come to an end.

‖ ‖ ‖ ‖ ‖ ‖

CHAPTER

1

Family Sabbath, 1938

THE TWENTY-FOUR HOURS between sunset on Friday and the appearance of the first star in the Polish sky on Saturday were dedicated to the name of the Eternal. It was the Sabbath, the most cherished image of Holiness, part of God's covenant with each Jew, to be carried by him throughout the ages in the pack on his back.

In our home in the city of Lvov the large dining table glowed with a white tablecloth. Usually eight, but this time nine, sets of festive china, crystal and silverware were laid on it, for my parents, my older sister Riwka, seven-year-old Rozia, my two younger brothers and me. There were also places for old Aaron, father's permanent oirach, or Saturday guest, and for a lone merchant who, caught away from his home, had been invited to have his Sabbath meal with us. According to the Torah, it is a mitzvah, a good deed, to bring an oirach home after the services in the synagogue.

The entire three-room apartment smelled of fresh wax, with which the maid Marusia had polished the oak parquet floors. Father put on his Hasidic Sabbath garb, a shiny black satin cloak and a strammel — a huge, round sable headgear — and bade Good Sabbath to his wife and children, just the way the Torah would have it.

We three brothers — Abo, Wilo, and myself Izio, were dressed in our Sabbath best, and wore Yarmulkas, small caps, on our heads, as we followed father as he walked slowly toward the Shul Hadushim, our synagogue, which was located two blocks from our home. Eight-year-old Wilo held my hand. I was the big brother; I was nineteen. The twelve-year-old Abo walked next to me.

The shul was crowded with adults who, like my father, wore Hasidic outfits. Their sons, similarly dressed, blended into the crowd of worshippers all in their black cloaks, with curled earlocks and pale, ascetic faces. We, the sons of reb Josef, or reb Yossel as he was known by most, stood out, for we were dressed in what were here considered outlandish European suits.

Father, who held the honorary position of gabbai, or a member of the shul's ritual elite, took a seat in the front row, with Wilo, in knee pants and long socks, at his side. Abo and I preferred to remain in the back. Surrounded by some of our Yeshivah and school friends, we would whisper and giggle and sneak out when father couldn't see us. We had a good time where we couldn't be considered a nuisance by our elders.

After the services, at home, my sister Riwka greeted us at the door. Twenty-four years old and unmarried, she was a young image of our beautiful mother. Only her silky blond hair gave a touch of Polishness to our very Jewish, very orthodox family.

Chava, our mother beamed with the grace of the Sabbath as she invited the guests to take seats. Immediately there ensued the usual fight between Rozia and Wilo, both of whom wanted to sit next to our parents. Father gave them one look of warning, and the tumult stopped.

Tantalizing aromas came from the kitchen into the dining room. Two huge, golden Challahs, soft and light white-bread loaves, lay on the table, soon to be blessed. I could tell from the odors that we were to have gefilte fish, wide slices of carp skin, filled with a mixture of chopped fish, onions, carrots, eggs, salt and pepper; and Chulent, the rich one-pot dish of beans, barley, potatoes, meat, and calf intestine stuffed with flour and fat—a unique Sabbath treat that had been cooking in the neighborhood baker's oven since Friday noon, now to be served, warm and tasty, as the main course. Last but not least there would be Tzimmes, a dessert made of carrots, cinnamon and honey.

Father said the Kiddush, the blessing of the wine, everybody washed his hands in the kitchen—a required pre-meal ritual—and all joined in saying the blessing of the Challahs. Dinner would be served by mother and Riwka. The Sabbath meal had begun.

Food was a serious matter, a gift the Almighty had

bestowed on man. It was to be consumed in pious silence, but during the intervals as empty plates were carried away and new courses brought in, father, his guests and his children softly chanted the Zmiroth, festive songs praising the Lord and His favorite day, the Sabbath. Serious as the occasion was, it was hard for me and my brothers to keep from laughing each time Abo's voice broke from a recently acquired baritone into a falsetto.

With the Tzimmes consumed, the Sabbath dinner reached its less formal phase. It was time for small talk.

"Nu? Father addressed the oirach Aaron. "How are things? How is your work? How is your Yekke son?" This was the Polish slang term for German Jew. Aaron's son had gone to Germany years before in search of a better life. He was his impoverished old father's favorite topic of conversation.

"Not so bad." Aaron replied. "Good. Everything is good." Aaron's most striking characteristic was his eternal optimism.

Father turned to his second guest, the merchant from a distant shtetl, small town. "And how are yours?"

"Thank God, my wife is healthy, my children are healthy, we are alive." What else could he say? The life of a small Jewish merchant in provincial Poland was seldom a thing to brag about.

Father's eyes now rested on me. Our weekly political duel was about to begin.

"So? Do you still feel that the Jews should boycott the general elections?"

I really wasn't sure what I felt. After all, there were a

few Jewish representatives in the Sejm, the Polish parliament, and we even had a few Jewish senators, most of them Zionists. I, too, was a Zionist—one of the movement's extreme right wing, a revisionist. I was a member of an organization called Betar, which brought attention to the need for the Jews to have a homeland in Palestine, by not taking part in Polish elections.

"We are against voting, because Poland is not our fatherland," I said solemnly. "Jews have been discriminated against for centuries. They have been murdered in pogroms right here in Lvov. When we're brutalized by the fascists, the authorities don't say boo. We belong in Palestine, in Eretz Yisroel, our true home."

"We'll belong in Eretz Yisroel when the Messiah comes and takes us there." As a Hasid, father wouldn't accept the idea of a Jewish homeland under any other conditions. "Meanwhile, we are what God made us to be. Pious Jews and good Poles."

This conversation might go on forever. Riwka nodded imperceptibly, giving me her mute approval. It was mother who finally intervened.

"It's all pusty reid," senseless chatter, she declared. "Why don't you take your friend Wolf," she added, addressing me directly, "and go for a walk with him to the Wysoki Zamek?"

I thought that was a good suggestion. Wysoki Zamek, the High Castle, was a man-made mound of earth a few hundred feet high turned into a park. It was the favorite meeting place for soldiers and housemaids, as well as the sons of Jewish families like mine.

"Baruch ata," father chanted — one last praise of God — as we lowered our eyes. This was the once-a-week occasion when we were closest to each other, and when, for a few hours, our home became an extension of the Land of Israel, a place with extra-territorial rights. No outside authority had a say here; father was the king and mother the queen.

CHAPTER

2

Daily Life in Lvov

"So, Judge Prachtel, tell me! What's going to happen? Will there be a war?"

It was small talk on an early-summer day in 1939. I was waiting for the judge to pay the monthly installment on some clothing and tapestries his wife had purchased at my family's shop. Checks were not yet in use; bills had to be collected in person and were paid in cash. The Prachtels, the Swirskis, and others, all Polish and Ukrainian professionals, high civil servants, army officers and businessmen, were our steady customers. They liked to do business with Uri Lichter and Family. We were honest merchants, and our prices and terms of payment could hardly be beaten.

The company bore my name, but its success was due

to mother's efforts. Raised in extremely orthodox surroundings, she had succeeded in crossing the ancient barriers. Taking correspondence courses, she had been able to graduate from the gymnasium, the rigorous European-style high school. Endowed with intelligence and organizational skills, she created a business that allowed my family to acquire two apartment houses, to educate the children in excellent schools and to have a respected style of life. My sister, Riwka, had completed courses in business administration. She took care of the firm's accounting. I was mother's right hand, her messenger and collector of installment payments at the age of fourteen, I was now, five years later, the company's outside man, its customer relations representative.

"What do you care whether there's war?" was the judge's comment. "Jews aren't fighting people. You won't be drafted."

Judge Prachtel was a decent Pole; he wasn't an anti-Semite. Yet even the nicest of Poles had little regard for the ability or willingness of their Jewish fellow-citizens to handle a rifle in defense of the fatherland. All Poles considered us cowards. They repeated it to us time and again until we began to believe it ourselves. They would say it in school to Jewish children, in the press to Jewish readers, in the streets of villages, towns and cities to Jewish masses. The Endeks, rabidly anti-Semitic university students, would tell it to us with sticks and stones, beating up Jews and smashing the windows of their stores. Poles like Judge Prachtel were satisfied with an occasional quip.

"I might be called to the army," I responded, pocketing the money. "I'll be just a private. I don't have to become an officer. Although I'm entitled to officer's training — I'm a gymnasium graduate."

The judge waved the possibility aside. "Stick to business. Our young men can take care of the Germans if Hitler dares to attack."

From that day in May 1939 when the head of the Polish army Marshal Rydz-Smigly went on the radio and promised the world that not one button of a Polish greatcoat would be surrendered to Hitler, war had been on everyone's lips. What the Nazis wanted, however, was not Polish buttons, but free and direct access to Danzig, the Baltic port. Between Germany and Danzig lay that much-disputed stretch of land known as the Polish Corridor. Danzig, now called Gdansk, is the modern port city that Poland had built as part of its dream of becoming a sea power.

War talk aside, life was normal. My family lived in a comfortable second-floor apartment in one of our two buildings in the section of Lvov where the Gentile and Jewish quarters met, at number 4 Zbozowa Street. To our east lay the choice area inhabited by Poles, Ukrainians and assimilated Jewish families. To the west, in the section known as "Behind the Theater," lived the orthodox Jews. Farther west, in dilapidated tenements, lived the poorest of the Jews. There, Polish, Ukrainian and Jewish thieves and streetwalkers had a comfortable hideaway seldom if ever visited by the law.

Around the corner, in a building next to ours, lived my girl friend Nesia. I had known the slender, dark-haired beauty since the days when I was a student in the gymnasium and she was enrolled in a private all-girl school. After graduating, she pursued her education at the Institute of International Commerce — a fact that created difficulties between us, since by my father's edict, I had to forego higher education.

Lvov was bustling with business. My father would start his day by putting on his phylacteries, prayer bands, wrapping himself in his tallit, prayer shawl, and reciting the morning prayers. These concluded, he'd don a black coat and a felt hat and, with a silver topped walking cane in hand, he'd head toward his usual business post — the bond and foreign-currency exchange, known in Yiddish as Die Berse. Actually, it was nothing more than a narrow dead-end street filled with Hasidic Jews in black hats and cloaks. Father would take a seat at a small table in the corner café, and discuss the price of the American dollar, over a cup of Viennese coffee.

Business at Die Berse was father's secondary occupation. The fifty-three-year-old son of a Talmudic scholar and grandson of a rabbi, he was a faithful disciple of the Belzer rebbe, and reb Yossel Lichter's real passion was the study of Talmud. He was so well versed in Halakha, the interpretations of the Scriptures, that, besides being a gabbai in the Shul Hadushim, he had been chosen by his Hasidic peers to be one of the three magistrates in the Din Torah. This was an informal but highly respected court where, in acknowledgement of the Mosaic tradition, ultra-orthodox Jews usually came to settle personal, and even business disputes.

A graduate of the Jewish gymnasium of Lvov, I had developed professional ambitions. I wanted to continue my education and become an architect. I had the necessary qualifications: a recognized gymnasium diploma, excellent knowledge of mathematics, even the ability to draft with either hand. My liabilities, though, outweighed my assets. There was a quota on the admission of Jews to the department of architecture in Lvov's polytechnic school. I overcame that hurdle by applying to the Technion in Haifa, that was when my father stepped in. "Enough schooling!" he declared. "You are my oldest son, and you belong in the business."

I suspected that mother would have liked me to be a professional, but she needed me. I was the one who made sure that the goods delivered were satisfactory. I was the one who collected the payments and the one all our customers liked and called "Mr. Izio."

CHAPTER

3

———

War

O<small>N</small> S<small>EPTEMBER</small> 1, 1939, the first German bombs burst
on Polish soil. Three weeks of bloody fighting followed. As
the dust of the battle settled, Germany and Russia divided
Poland once again and the eastern part of the country,
including Lvov, became a province of the Soviet Union.

The beginning of the occupation was marked by utter
chaos as well as by jokes about the members of the Red
Army — terribly unsophisticated people, if not downright
primitive. One could see them everywhere, as they and
the refugees from Nazi-occupied western Poland crowded
the streets of Lvov. Akademicka Street, a main artery
known informally as the Corso, was bursting with out-of-

towners, some of them Jewish bourgeoisie from Warsaw, whose female folk could be recognized by their shearling coats and elegant boots — a bow to what was considered the Russian fashion.

Officers and soldiers of the Red Army and civilian Poles, Ukrainians and Jews jostled one another in the crowded Corso. But the Russians didn't really mingle; it was as though they felt out of place in this metropolis where East and West met. They wore greatcoats which almost covered their felt boots — leather was scarce in the Soviet Union. Most of the Russian women were clad like their men, but now and then a blond young female would be seen who boasted a dress made of sheer fabric, thus putting herself in double jeopardy by wearing an outfit better suited to the bedroom than to the Corso, where the temperature ran in the low teens.

Pasaz Mikolasza, a glass-enclosed mall at the corner of Marjacki Square and Legionow Street, had been lined before the war with inexpensive variety stores, a pharmacy and two second-rate movie houses. Now it housed a thriving black market where local hustlers kept busy trying to satisfy the Red Army's taste for the four products it desired most ardently — watches, leather boots, vodka and women. One could stand for hours and watch as bundles of worthless rubles changed hands for those items. At the top of the list were watches. One could often see a hustler, as he'd shake a timepiece with a broken spindle and loose parts near the ear of a Soviet buyer, hypnotizing him with the incantation, "Can you hear that splendid tick-tock?" In the throng, a Mongol-faced soldier might pull up the sleeve of his coat and flaunt a dark-skinned arm adorned with a half dozen watches, bought because they were a rare commodity in his homeland.

As for women, the streetwalkers of Lvov soon became the object of unusual interest on the part of the occupying army. However, during the early months of 1940, the women disappeared from the corners. Local gossip had it that most of them had become the duly wedded spouses of lucky Soviet army men.

The poorest of the Jews, people who had spent most of their lives in the worst tenements of the "Behind the Theater" quarter, emerged now in the Gentile section of Lvov. For the first time in their lives they dared respond when pushed aside by a Pole in an overcrowded streetcar, and to snap, "Simmer down! Your genteel Poland is dead!" The Poles of Lvov never forgot these taunts, and all the city's Jews would one day be held accountable for the behavior of those few.

In Polish eyes, every Jew had suddenly become a Communist.

Assimilated Jews as well as the orthodox ones found themselves in a vise. Poles had lost all consideration for their Jewish compatriots, if they had ever had any, and the Russians were too occupied with themselves to offer any.

Soon after the take-over of the eastern half of Poland by the Russians, their Security Police, NKVD, opened a headquarters in Lvov. Its arm was long and ruthless.

Russian control over the life of the residents began with the introduction of an identity document — a passport. One by one, long-time residents as well as the refugees from western Poland were ordered to report to the nearest police precinct. There, each one's occupation and social status was examined, after which a determination was made: identity document or deportation.

Rumors had it that Nazi spies had infiltrated among the refugees from German-occupied Poland. The NKVD made a practical decision: better a thousand innocent people in Siberia than one spy in Lvov. Trucks or horse-drawn wagons stopped in front of buildings where refugees lived, and unwanted strangers were dragged out and taken to the Podzamcze railroad terminal. There they were herded into boxcars in which they waited, cold and hungry, sometimes for several days, for the trip to Siberia.

Once the status of the refugees was settled, it was the turn of the permanent residents of Lvov who were considered bourgeoisie. Under Paragraph Eleven of the relevant Soviet law, industrialists, land owners, landlords and merchants were denied identity documents. Such people faced either deportation to Siberia or exile to one of the small towns east of the city. My family and I found ourselves subject to Paragraph Eleven and we were consigned to an eastern small town.

We left the city. We left our comfortable apartment and most of our furniture. For the first time, we had a taste of how hard it was to live in Russian Poland.

For the next few months we lived in Zborow, a tiny town not far from the old Russian border. Here the inhabitants were mostly Jewish. In Shalom Aleichem's books, Zborow would be described as a shtetl in the Pale of Settlement. The Pale was the only area where a Jew might live. From there, we corresponded with a Jewish woman, a tenant for many years on the third floor of our building in Lvov. She was so poor that my mother, instead of asking her to pay rent, had often given her and her four children, food for Passover and Rosh Hashanah so that she and her family would not go hungry during the high holidays. Now, my mother's kindness paid off. The woman's son-in-law, an old-time Communist who had suffered much under the Polish regime, had become a man of importance in the Soviet hierarchy. With the permission of his superiors, he locked our apartment and kept it intact as he negotiated our return to the city. After six months we received our passports and returned to Lvov.

Back home, I visited each of our old customers. Many of them owed us money. I knew that very few in Lvov were able to pay; more than anything else, these visits were a sort of customer relations exercise.

"How are you doing?" I asked Mrs. Prachtel.

"Not too well," she replied. "They deported my husband."

A prominent man before the war, and a nationalist, Judge Prachtel had fallen victim to the NKVD, along with many Polish army officers and some major political figures.

"I'm very sorry," I said. "Sincerely sorry."

"I know you are. You were always nice. But now I have a problem." She blushed. "I don't have the money to pay the installment. Maybe it would be best if you repossessed the goods."

"Please, don't worry." I was embarrassed as well. "Sooner or later, times will change. Everything will return to normal. Judge Prachtel will be back, and you'll pay us then."

I did not know when things would change. I wasn't sure if they ever would. People owed us a lot of money, about 800,000 zloty, or $150,000 in today's dollars, but nobody could pay. The Soviet authorities had frozen bank deposits a few days after they seized eastern Poland, and a couple of days later allowed the depositors to withdraw only 500 zloty worth of rubles per family. Whoever had money in the bank lost most of it. Those who kept it at home in a stocking had no way to convert it to rubles. Only those who had American dollars or gold coins could continue to live near normally. "Not to worry" became my standard response to customers. With that, I earned their respect and gratitude — intangible assets which would prove priceless a few years later.

Once a full-time business woman, mother now became a hard-pressed housewife. Trying to make ends meet, even with help from Riwka, was hard. Though far better off than most of the small towns to the east, Lvov had its food shortages. Bread, milk, butter, cheese, vegetables, cooking oil, meat and other staples disappeared from the market, and could be acquired from the Ukrainian peasants only through barter. People would line up in front of bakeries at two in the morning. If they were lucky, they might be able to buy half a loaf of soggy, heavy, rye bread six hours later. Ironically, at the same time, recently opened Soviet food stores offered unlimited amounts of red caviar at five rubles per pound or the choicest black caviar for ten rubles. One could also buy a cheap canned shellfish called snatka, and coarse salt by the bag.

As before the war, I was mother's right hand. In

exchange for clothing, I obtained flour, kasha, beans, onions, vegetables and cooking oil from the peasants, and our cold apartment once again smelled like home. On entering, we would be engulfed by the odors of good food, previously the aromatic sign of well-to-do Jewishness in eastern Europe.

Under Soviet law, those who didn't work didn't eat. Thus, everybody had to have a job, or at least a slip of paper certifying that the bearer was employed. Such certificates were easily bought, and no one was overly curious whether the bearer actually worked. In this way we continued living, hoping that sooner or later the war — thus far confined to Germany and western Europe — would end. Nations would sober up, the Russians would retreat to their old borders, and I could start collecting the money our customers owed us.

Then something unexpected happened: at dawn on June 22, 1941, Lvov awoke to the explosions of bombs falling over the city. We turned on the radio and heard the Nazi minister of propaganda, Joseph Goebbels, announce that Germany had embarked on a crusade against the godless Bolsheviks.

It was not the denouement we had expected. The future we'd had in mind was much simpler: Germany defeated by the Allies, goodbye Stalin, and long live Poland. This would be a new Poland, of course, where a Jew would finally be considered a Mensch, a normal human being. It was not to be.

Coming out of shelter after one of the waves of Nazi bombers had passed over the city, I came across the imprint, in fresh asphalt outside the veterinary school, of a bomb. The bomb itself was gone — destroyed, taken away, I don't know. Only the dent in the pavement remained; its image has stayed with me as the first tangible sign of the advancing night of terror.

CHAPTER

4

———

Nazi Terror in Lvov

J UNE 30, 1941: Hitler's troops had just captured Lvov (the Germans called it Lemberg).

The horrors started in early July with what came to be known in the history of the modern Jewish Diaspora as the Petlura Days. In a blind rage, the uniformed members of the Ukrainian Brigade, a part of the invading German army, accompanied by the local nationalist rabble, chased 3,000 Jews to the Brygitki prison and to the Piaski, or Sand Mountain, and there murdered them with machine guns, rifles and prosaic iron bars. Soon, we would feel the Angel of Death over our own household. In November of that year, Riwka was abducted by the SS, from the shop where she worked. Along with other young women, she was herded into one of the deportation trucks and shipped away. She was never heard from again.

From that time on, Jewish life was uninterrupted humiliation, persecution and suffering. What had begun as mob fury turned into a carefully planned, though not meticulously executed, genocide.

One block away from us lived our cousin Shmuel with his family. Shmuel's wife, Machla, was our mother's first cousin, but we always considered Shmuel our cousin as well.

We had all co-existed peacefully with Polish and Ukrainian families, many of them were good customers and gracious acquaintances. Then double lightning — the SS, struck the Jews of Lvov. In November, the month Riwka was taken from us, a German edict hit those Jews who lived in the Gentile part of the city. They were ordered to relocate immediately to the area behind the great theater, the section which before the war had been populated by the poorest of Jews. As soon as the more genteel part of Lvov had been emptied of Jews, it was dubbed the Aryan Quarter, and the first official pogrom — something the Germans referred to as Umsiedlung, resettlement or simply the Action — took place.

On a gloomy morning, we heard the first sounds of the Umsiedlung. Police kicked at our door and pounded it with rifle butts. I tried to stay calm. I ordered mother and the younger children, Wilo and Rozia, to slip under the covers of the feather bed. I told Abo to cram into a corner of the balcony. Then I shoved the heavy wooden wardrobe over the entrance to it, so that a stranger to the apartment might not guess what was behind.

The intruders, meanwhile, pushed their way in and confronted me as I was finally about to open the door for them. A German Schupo man, or policeman, slapped my face sharply.

"You son of a bitch!" he bawled. "Why didn't you open up immediately? Where are the other Jewish swine hiding?"

He held me against the wall, as three of his men, one German, one Ukrainian and one Jewish policeman, searched the apartment. Within seconds, they found our father in the dining room and Abo on the balcony, the imposing wardrobe notwithstanding. Lined up against the wall, each was administered the regulation slap in the face, after which the Jewish lawman stepped forward. I knew him. He had been my teammate on the Hasmonea, a Jewish soccer team.

"Where are your mother and the two children?" he asked in a commanding voice.

It was an unbelieveable scene, something to which we weren't yet accustomed: a Jew selling out another Jew.

"You can't mean it!" I appealed desperately to the myth of brotherhood among Jews. "You know what happens to people who get deported!"

"I mean it," he repeated glacially. "Where is the old woman? Where are the children?"

I managed to regain my composure. "I don't know," I said quietly. "Nowadays, it's everyone for himself. They must be hiding somewhere in town."

"Alle 'raus!" shouted the German. "Everybody out!"

We were chased out to the street and into an open truck now filled to capacity with Jewish hostages.

I realized that some action was required if our lives were to be saved. I stepped forward and addressed the German guard: "Ich melde mich gehorsam!" That phrase — "I obediently report!" — would become my slogan of survival, the first step in persuading or, if need be, bribing, a German or Ukrainian jailer. "That man over there," I said, pointing to my father, "is an important specialist in a Wehrmacht detail. You've got to let him go."

I will never know whether the guard was more impressed by my knowledge of German or by my chutzpah. Perhaps he was simply a decent man. Whatever the case, suddenly father was off the truck of the damned. Abo and I were still on it.

Each of the Jewish men and women with us on the truck carried a bundle of belongings. Impressed, perhaps, by my success with the guard, they wanted me to tell them where we were going. Was it really to the city of Lublin, as the Germans were saying? I didn't know, of course, though I feared a fate worse than resettlement. I didn't linger to speculate. I motioned to Abo, and we jumped off the truck as it moved slowly through the crowded, winding streets of the Jewish quarter. We simply walked away! No one ordered us to return or shot at us. That evening, our family was reunited in our apartment.

Shortly after this episode father made a startling announcement. Everyone looked at him expectantly. "God forgive me," the old man said, his voice choking as he caressed his long, silky beard. "I have decided to shave off my beard and my payus," earlocks. "It is necessary if I want to be free to leave the apartment and move about."

This was a relief. Father's appearance had become a life-threatening liability, but none of us would have dared suggest that he shave off the facial hair he considered a symbol of his religious status. He really had no choice, for the beard and the earlocks would attract the attention of any German soldier.

During another Nazi Action, in March 1942, father was caught again. His Kennkarte, identity and working paper, was confiscated, and he was thrown, with a large group of other Jews, into the Sobieskiego, an elementary school converted to a deportation center.

At that time, we all worked for the Ryzewskyj Kaserne Renovierungsbüro. This was a construction and repair firm owned by a Mr. Ryzewskyj, a turncoat Polish Ukrainian who before the war had been a steady customer of our business. He still owed us money. We also knew Ryzewskyj's chief engineer and office manager, a Mr. Baranskyj, himself a Ukrainian and now my immediate superior. Baranskyj's carried a lot of weight with the owner, who had an unusually unattractive niece. He hoped, one day, she would become Mrs. Baranskyj.

As soon as we learned of father's predicament, I focused attention on Baranskyj and eventually got him to help me. The two of us went to Sobieskiego to help father.

The courtyard and the interior of the school were filled with Jews; men, women and children. They were frightened—nobody knew, as yet, the exact meaning of an SS Action. Still, everyone realized that it was better to remain hungry at home than travel with German and Ukrainian police to what the authorities liked to call resettlement in purely Jewish territory, somewhere near Lublin. It was not easy for me to point out only my father and his best friend, and to shut my eyes to the rest. But a first rule of survival is: save yourself first, and then, if you can, help others.

As for Baranskyj, he did more than his standards required, by asking for the release of both father and his friend.

Then came the great resettlement of August 1942, and with it the savage destruction of the Jewry of Lvov. The Judenrath, a German-created Council of the Elders for the Jewish community, was disbanded. Half of its members were hanged, and the rest were put into the recently organized Janowska labor camp. This was tantamount to a death sentence. A ghetto was officially instituted to keep tabs on us and large scale deportations went on for days.

At first, Wilo and Rozia hid along with eight other people in the neighborhood bakery, behind the oven walls. After a few stifling days, the children in the group, half-naked and confused, were led to another shelter: the cesspool in the courtyard of our building. The tank housed twenty-five people, mostly children and older men and women from the neighborhood. As the turmoil continued, mother, too, found her way there.

Father, Abo and I remained in our apartment, hoping that the deportations would stop. For the moment, we felt fairly safe, being employed by Ukrainian companies that had contracts with the German army. At this point father and Abo worked for Kuczko Canalization, a sewer and cesspool subcontractor for the Ryzewskyj firm. Each of us had a patch with a capital "W" stamped on it and a Star of David arm band, a generally accepted, though not always honored, worker's I.D. My position was strategic. I had become Ryzewskyj's transportation foreman, and, as such traveled on a horse-drawn wagon. I made it my business to pass by our home once a day, so I could hurriedly thrust a sackful of bread into the cesspool to keep mother and the children, and some of the others, from dying of hunger.

As days passed, the deportations increased. The streets of the ghetto became shooting galleries for crazed German and Ukrainian police, and my task became increasingly difficult.

Across from our building was a large open lot bordered at one end by a high concrete wall. In the old days there had been a flea market in the lot, and at that time it bore the name of Platz Solski. Now it was a gathering place for Jews rounded up by the SS and the Ukrainian police. From there, open trucks would transport their human loads to the Janowska labor camp, where the new arrivals were either put to forced labor or murdered. Sometimes, they were spared the agony of waiting: the victims would be shot beside the Platz Solski wall, a site that, appropriately, came to be known as the Wailing Wall.

Returning on foot from work to our home one never to be forgotten August evening, I was confronted with a scene like one out of Hieronymus Bosch, who was the Flemish painter of damned souls. A half drunk SS Sturmfürher with a Luger in his right hand stood in the courtyard, yelling, "Raus! Stinkende Jüdische Schweinehunde!" Half a dozen Ukrainian policemen in black uniforms leveled their rifles on the people as they climbed out of the cesspool one by one, dripping with water and excrement, much like Bosch's malodorous devils. Moaning as they were beaten with rifle butts, they were pushed into the small back yard and stood up against the wall of the building. "You stinking Jewish pigs! Raus! Raus!" the Sturmfürher kept roaring, as more and more men, women and children crowded up against each other and the wall.

As this was taking place, Abo and father returned from work. Two Ukrainian policemen stopped them at the entrance of our building and questioned them briefly. They allowed Abo to go upstairs, but confiscated father's documents and dispatched him to the courtyard.

Abo felt helpless and desperate. I could see him through the apartment window as he grabbed a long kitchen knife. I rushed upstairs and found him shaking. "I'll kill those murderers! he cried. "I'll kill at least one of them before they murder my family!"

"Don't be foolish, Abo," I said. "Put the knife away. This isn't the answer."

I hurried back downstairs, snapped to attention in front of the drunken SS officer, and announced crisply, "Herr Sturmfürher! Ich melde mich gehorsam!" Pointing to father, I added, "That man there works for me. I'm his foreman."

The SS man was caught by surprise. Perhaps for the first time in his life, he had seen a bold Jew. After a moment of hesitation, he ordered the Ukrainians to release the old man. I hissed to father in Yiddish, "Disappear! And stay away from the apartment!"

Now the Sturmfürher began to evaluate me.

"Do you live in this building?" he asked, pointing directly to our apartment. "Yes," I said, and played for time. "Please, won't you come in?"

As we entered the apartment, the officer turned to the Ukrainian guard who trailed us and barked, "You! Stay outside the door!" Once inside, the flushed and glassy-eyed officer, hardly in control of his body, fell heavily to a chair and, ominously, set his revolver down on the dining room table.

"Hast du Schnapps?" he ordered. "Do you have anything to drink?"

Fortunately, I was able to produce a full bottle of vodka and two glasses.

"What do you want from me?" the SS man said as he filled both glasses. With a broad gesture, he invited me to help myself to one. "Prosit!" he added, gulping his own.

"Please, Herr Sturmfürher, let my people go free," I begged.

"And who might your people be?"

"My mother and my kid brother and sister."

"Do you have any gold?" He was proposing an exchange.

"I do," I lied. I knew that Shmuel had gold coins, and that he would not refuse to help.

"Put it on the table."

"It's not in the house. It'll take me five minutes to get it."

"Then hurry!"

I ran to Shmuel's. There, I described the situation to

his wife, and soon, I was back with a handful of Czarist gold rubles. It couldn't have taken me more than five minutes, but it seemed like an eternity.

"Here it is!" Breathless, I laid the rubles on the table.

The German was well into the vodka. He yelled drunkenly at the guard while pocketing the money: "You, Ukrainian pig! Open the door and come here."

The guard snapped to attention at the threshold. "Take this man downstairs," the officer continued. "He'll pick out several people from the crowd, and you'll let them go."

Thus I was able to save the lives of mother, Wilo, Rozia and even a man and a child, who were neighbors. I repeated to them what I had told father: "Get away from here! Don't come back to the house for several hours!" I then returned to the apartment, where the Sturmfürher was still waiting. Abo was in the next room hiding.

"I don't think you're a Jew," the SS man commented as he drank another glass of vodka. "You can't be. You don't look like a Jew. Well-dressed, blond." I remained silent. "Maybe we could do some more business. Do you have more gold? Do you have more relatives in that group?"

"Yes," I said. "Yes to gold, and yes to relatives."

"Then go and get me more coins, and I'll have some more of your people freed."

Before I could turn to leave, the door was thrown open and two Ukrainian policemen dragged in a screaming middle-aged woman. Disheveled and reeking of the cesspool, she threw herself at the German's feet. Clinging to his boots and kissing the shiny leather, she sobbed for mercy; as he pushed her back with his foot, she added, "If

I'm taken away, then I want the Lichter woman and her children deported too! Otherwise there's no justice. If I go, let them go with me!"

The Sturmfürher kicked her in the face, stood up, picked up his Luger and said to me, "These are your God damn Jews! They aren't worth gold. They're shit." He ordered the Ukrainians to take the woman away, then paused and turned to me.

"The Lichter woman is your mother, isn't she?"

"Yes."

"Where is she? Where are the children that woman mentioned?"

"I don't know, Herr Sturmfürher. I just don't know. They aren't here. Maybe they've already been resettled."

The officer waved with indifference; he probably thought that every Jew would go sooner or later. Without again mentioning more gold and more people to be freed, he stumbled out of the apartment. In the back yard, he shot once into the air as though to remind those who might have forgotten that he was in charge, and ordered everyone still there, onto the trucks.

Two days later, on August 28, 1942, the summer Action ended. From the Nazi point of view, it had been a complete success. Between the SS Vernichtungskommando, the Extermination Detail, and the Gestapo, the Schupo, the Ukrainian police and, last but not least, Ukrainian and Polish collaborators, 50,000 Jews had been "resettled."

On September 7, a new edict ordered the remaining Jews to move into a substantially reduced area of the ghetto, a pale enclosed within recently erected high concrete walls that bordered two of the city's poorest neighborhoods, Kleparowska and Zamarstynowska Streets.

Our family, along with Shmuel and his wife and son, moved into a poor dilapitated house on Kleparowska Street. Two small rooms and a kitchen had to accommodate nine people—a far cry from our previous style of life. However, our new residence offered one luxury we didn't have in our old building. This was a potato pit in the center of the kitchen, a potential hiding place. All we had to do was board it up in such a way that no one could see the difference between the old floor planks and the new ones.

In the meantime, even though the remaining Jews continued working for the firms that aided the German war effort and there was no official Action, Nazi and Ukrainian patrols kept hunting Jewish children, old people and the sick. In November, the number of SS forces and Ukrainian police patrolling the ghetto rose sharply, and thus we knew that a new mass Action was about to befall us. Since father, Abo and I were employed, it was mother, Wilo and Rozia about whom we had to worry.

The day the new Action began, mother and the children slipped down into the potato pit; Abo, father and I covered the opening with a plank and pushed a heavy wooden chest over it. Father and Abo then left for work, leaving me behind to take care of the finishing touches.

When I went out myself, I felt a wave of anxiety. As though possessed, I heard a continuous wailing from the kitchen; unable to withstand the tension, I rushed back. As I entered the kitchen I heard faint, but real, complaints from beneath the floor. Now frantic, I shoved the chest aside, a feat that a few hours earlier had required three people, and uncovered the pit.

Mother and Wilo were near suffocation, and little Rozia had lost consciousness. I splashed them with water and prayed for their survival. Mother was the first to come to. "Where are the children?" was her immediate worry. Wilo was the next to open his eyes. Then came Rozia's turn. However, the child remained in a state of shock for several days. The experience had been too great a trauma for the ten-year-old; she was not up to a life of stealth and hiding, and a different solution would have to be found for her.

As the November Action eased and normal ghetto life resumed, we concentrated our thoughts on Rozia. "The only way to save her is for her to stay with a Polish family," I said, and the others agreed. I was to make the arrangements. As the former customer relations man for our business, I had come into contact with people at the highest level of Polish society in Lvov. One of them might be willing to help.

"I'll go to Mrs. Prachtel," I decided. The judge's wife had offered to help us when the Germans had first captured Lvov. Disguised as best I could to look like a Pole, I visited her and her daughter, told them about our little sister and asked for help. Mrs. Prachtel's response was an immediate "yes."

When I arrived home I spoke with my parents and told them that the Prachtels had willingly agreed to hide Rozia.

Explaining to Rozia proved to be difficult. We had to explain to a ten year old child, that to save her life, she would have to leave her loved ones and live with a strange Polish family. Rozia's reluctance to leave us was made more difficult by the great emotion none of us could contain.

The burden of separation weighed heaviest on my mother, who was now in danger of losing her second and youngest daughter.

That evening, I took Rozia by the hand, clambered through an opening in the ghetto wall — an escape route that had frequently been used by other fleeing Jews — and delivered her with a bundle of personal necessities to the Prachtels. From then on, Rozia would be a Polish child, Halina Korecka — a niece of Mrs. Prachtel, according to the papers I forged for her.

On January 7, 1943, the Lvov ghetto was once again decimated. The Jewish community of the city, once one hundred sixty thousand souls, had now been reduced to fifteen thousand. The residential quarter had shrunken to a few miserable streets lined with overcrowded tenement houses, the whole surrounded by a wall with one gate. A new name was given to this area: Das Judenlager, the Jewish Camp. Children were forbidden to live in that horrible place, as were men and women who were unable to obtain a work permit, the treasured Arbeitskarte. Though the city was under Nazi control, the Marxist law of "he who doesn't work, doesn't eat" still ruled, and anyone able to move toiled in one capacity or another. Workers also needed the Jewish arm band and a patch with the letter "W" for Wehrmacht or "R" for Rustung, armaments industry, prominently displayed.

Ours was now a family of five, each of us employed by Ryzewskyj or one of its sub-contractors. Father and Abo labored for Kuczko's; Wilo, now thirteen, was an apprentice for the Satz group, a plumbing-repair outfit. As the head of Ryzewskyj's transportation detail, I was stable master in charge of three nags and three wagons and, with two other drivers, hauled construction material to various sites. Even mother had a job. She managed Ryzewskyj's community kitchen, where a group of Jewish women prepared a meager evening meal for the Jews who were forced to work without pay.

Every firm working for the German military machine had a building assigned to it where its Jewish employees had to live. Ryzewskyj was given a three-story structure near Zamarstynowska Street. From our window, we could see the Aryan Quarter. But we could also see the Special Detail of the SS and the Ukrainian police, who were there to ensure that the compound was escape-proof.

My horse and wagon were a unique blessing for our family. Since in it, I was mobile, I could turn a gold coin or a piece of jewelry that mother would no longer wear into the most precious commodity of the era, food. A bottle of Schnapps hidden in the wagon served as a discreet payment for a laissez-passer from the guards at the gate. The extra food I supplied was particularly important because we were trying, under the most difficult circumstances, to cling to the law of kashruth, to eat only kosher foods.

Jews were not allowed to leave their quarter individually. They could leave in work details early in the morning, marching to the music of the "Beer Barrel Polka" played by a Jewish band at the gate. The jaunty lyrics — "My Mlodzi!

My Mlodzi! Nam bimber nie zaszkodzil!" "We're young! We're young! A glass of Schnapps won't hurt us!" — were presumably considered a good spur for languishing marchers.

Each morning, as the details passed through the gate on their way to work, Obersturmbannfürher Grzymek, a lieutenant colonel clad in the gray and black SS uniform, stood on a platform, surrounded by a retinue of German and Ukrainian guards. Now and then he poked a thick finger at one of the people marching past. That finger had the power of life or death, or, if he was in a benign mood, that of a solid lashing. Occasionally he'd thumb out one of the Jews and order a Ukrainian to administer his personal "one for the road" — ten or twenty lashes. After that, the detail would be permitted to continue on its way.

One morning in April 1943, it was my turn. Flogged by a Ukrainian policeman, I bit my lower lip and tried to endure the pain. Why had I been picked? Slim and of medium height, I didn't have any particular trait that would attract Herr Grzymek's eye unless it was the mustache I'd grown. It had reached a respectable size and shape. Under different circumstances, I believed, the mustache would make me look Polish, or even downright German. Instead, the way things were, I was simply a young Jew from the Judenlager with a black and blue behind.

Ryzewskyj's Aryan representative, one of the Ukrainian foremen, took charge of our detail outside the gate and marched us to the firm's headquarters on Kolontaja Street. As we walked, I considered the latest developments. I was fed up with being forced to live in sub-human conditions. I wanted to be able to forget the threat of sudden murder that hung over the remnants of the Jewish community of Lvov.

As though he could read my thoughts, a man came to the kitchen that evening with electrifying news. He had escaped from the Janowska camp and now, as he stayed with us for Passover, he spoke of his brother in law, an old neighbor of ours and a pre-war teammate of mine on the Hasmonea soccer team. Once known by his Jewish name, Shmuel, he had lately assumed the Russian name Kolya, and with his gentile looks and phony Ukrainian papers had already traveled several times between Lvov and Dnepropetrovsk, an industrial city in the southeast Ukraine some eight hundred kilometers from the Judenlager.

"Kolya said he's done it a number of times," I whispered to my family a few evenings later. Although we were at home, everyone spoke softly; in the Judenlager, there was no way of knowing if we could be overheard. "For some money and an exchange of services he'll get me a train ticket and an official permit to add to my Polish I.D. papers to go to Dnepropetrovsk. On this trip, he's taking a woman and four men; in all, we'll be seven. He'll be the foreman. We'll be Polish laborers assigned to build roads for a German construction company near the eastern front."

"What kind of services can you offer to Kolya?" father asked.

"I'll make him counterfeit printer's stamps."

Everyone knew my talent for drawing. I had already

used my skills to produce identity papers for Rozia Halina. I was ambidextrous, and there wasn't a signature that I couldn't reproduce.

Father continued his questioning. "What will you use to make the stamps?"

"Potatoes. They're the usual material to use for counterfeit rubber stamps."

"So, if you can do all those things, why don't you do what other Jews are doing? Why don't you go to Warsaw? Go west, and you'll be closer to the Americans and the British. Don't you think it's ridiculous to head east? It's filled with Germans and what's worse, Ukrainians. There are a million people in Warsaw—nobody would notice you."

"Warsaw is too dangerous if I'm identified as a Jew," I replied. "That's why I should go to Dnepropetrovsk. I'll be safe there. It's in the eye of the storm."

Father pondered the matter. "You know what?" he said. "I like the idea. It's poetic."

Father's opinion was tantamount to a blessing. In a few moments, however, I began to have second thoughts.

"I can't leave you just to save my own skin," I said. Father was clearly moved. Still, he responded with a lighthearted comment, a Jewish saying coined in corrupted Polish: "Caly Lvov na twoj glow!"—in effect, "You can't save everyone in Lvov." "Don't worry," he added. "Go with Kolya. We'll manage. It will make things easier to think that one of our sons might survive to carry on the family name. Go, and God bless you."

"All right, I'll go," I agreed. "But I want you to know

that I'll be back. I'll get all of you out of this wretched place."

I stroked my mustache. I felt a little like a minor league Moses who had pledged to God and to himself to lead this one family of Jews out of this twentieth-century Egypt, toward an unknown promised land.

╫ ╫ ╫ ╫ ╫ ╫

CHAPTER

5

———

Learning to Live

in Nazi-Occupied Russia

At the end of April 1943, I stopped being Izio Lichter.
I became Pan Stanislaw Nowak, a true Pole, one entitled to
use the old Polish appelation for master—or an ethnic
German. In a last act of separation, I took off my Jewish
arm band and hid it in Ryzewskyj's kitchen along with my
Kennkarte, my identification card, and any other remaining symbols of my enslavement and my Jewishness.

Kolya's group was scheduled to meet in one of the
several Rohstofferfassung depots, an old warehouse that
smelled of soiled clothing and all kinds of old uniforms that
the Germans collected for repairs and recycling. The en-

trance to the building was off a narrow alley — a dead end called Karna Street. It was desolate, and a perfect hiding place for a few scared Jews on the run.

Dressed in my best leather jacket and carrying a small rucksack, I cautiously pushed the side door open. The sound it made scared me fully.

"You're late!" Kolya's angry whisper reached me from behind a pile of old Wehrmacht uniforms. In almost total darkness I groped my way toward the voice. Kolya, a young woman, and two men of about my age sat on bundles of clothes, each with a knapsack on his or her lap.

Indeed, I was late — by fifteen minutes or so. I didn't know why Kolya had to make such a thing of it, considering that we still had to wait more than an hour for the pick-up van. He had arranged for it to take us to the main railroad terminal in the northwestern part of the city. There, we were supposed to catch our train.

Finally, the van arrived. We crammed into the back. The Polish driver locked the door; then, with Kolya sitting beside him, he stepped on the gas and we were off.

Fifteen minutes later the van stopped. The driver opened the door and two more men climbed in. I had just enough time to catch a glimpse of the building from which they had emerged, probably another warehouse, before the door was shut.

The night was dark and cool, and a fine, bone-chilling rain was falling, typical early-spring weather in what had once been eastern Poland.

All of a sudden we veered and stopped short. I could hear the driver curse, "The son of a bitch has a flat tire!"

Kolya ranted, "Couldn't have happened in a worse place. Right in front of the Wehrmacht barracks!"

My heart hammered. I couldn't see anything from inside the van, but there was no way to ignore the sound of thumping of the German guard's boots. As the driver was busy replacing the tire, the guard marched back and forth, passing close to the van about every five minutes. Each time I heard him approach, I thought, "This is it. Now he's going to rip the door open and yell, 'Heraus, you damned Jews!' "Somehow I felt, from the moment I discarded my arm band, that every Gentile alive had focused his attention on me.

Fortunately, I was wrong. Perhaps it was because of the nasty weather but the sentry never bothered to stop and inquire. The van finally started again for the railroad station. There, the driver let us out, got his fee from Kolya and left us.

Though there were seven of us, we felt very lonely. We were surrounded by darkness and soaked by the rain; most painful was the fact that the flat tire had made us miss our train.

"We are late by ten minutes," Kolya announced.

"What do we do now?" a pair of fear-stricken voices inquired. "Maybe somebody knows a Gentile who will let us spend the night in his place—for a price?"

"No!" This was the moment for Kolya to display his leadership. "We'll head toward the Lewandowka station right now." That was in the northeastern part of Lvov. "If we're lucky, we will catch our train there."

We marched through the rain. I don't know how long it took us to reach Lewandowka, but when we finally arrived, our train was gone. Kolya explained to the Polish stationmaster that we were with the Organization Todt, that we were expected in Dnepropetrovsk and that we needed a lift on a freight train going east. Impossible, said the stationmaster; it was illegal for a freight train carrying military equipment to take on passengers. The best advice he could offer was to return to the main terminal and catch the morning express from there.

Now we were depressed as well as frightened. We were stuck in the middle of nowhere, the night was darker than ever, and we were cold and wet.

"Right now, the most important thing is not to be spotted by the police or a military patrol," Kolya whispered. "Let's get to the watchtower down by the track. It looks abandoned."

We followed the leader and crowded into the empty tower. There, trembling with cold and fear, we waited for dawn, hoping that a new day would bring a solution to our predicament.

Before sunrise, we began our tramp from Lewandowka back to the main station. In my expensive-looking leather jacket, I fantasized that I resembled a halutz, a youthful emigrant to Palestine. As a group, we probably resembled a troop of overgrown scouts carrying our packs on a field trip. Kolya was the scoutmaster, responsible for our present misery and future success.

We marched and marched. It rained, it seemed, interminably. Soon after daybreak we reached the terminal, the Wiener Bahnhof, the Vienna Railway Station, the main railroad station in Lvov.

Kolya ordered us to split into three groups of two, to

make ourselves less conspicuous. But, first he went inside the station with our documents, to get our clearance to buy our tickets to board the train.

I didn't like waiting in front, on the broad steps of the building. So we took seats on the nearest bench across from the station entrance from there we could watch the huge clock on the station's facade. I had the distinct impression that the clock didn't move at all. My eyes were then drawn to the imposing nose of my companion Zachar, and to his Basque beret. Between his nose and his beret he looked like a Frenchman.

A shoeshine boy who had decided that Zachar's shoes required his services began to plague us. He insisted on polishing those shoes most energetically. My companion took out a handkerchief and pretending to have an attack of hay fever, he committed his nose to its shelter. The shoeshine boy could be dangerous, as the Nazis promised a bounty to any successful informant. If the boy suspected that we were Jewish, or if we acted frightened, he might report us.

A little later, several Ukrainian policemen arrived. One of them had a German shepherd dog, but luckily the dog could not smell the difference between a Jew and an Aryan. We decided it was time to change our location, and we moved to another bench. It was better situated, since it hid us from casual view but permitted us a clear view of the station entrance.

At nine a.m. the ordeal ended. Kolya emerged from the station smiling, paused on the landing, and winked at us. He had everything: travel permits, tickets, and last but not least, a surge of new found courage. The train was to leave in fifteen minutes, so like obedient boy scouts we trotted behind our guide.

The main terminal of Lvov was the first serious hurdle for any Jew intent on fleeing the city. Swarming with people as in the pre-war days, it stimulated the excitement of travel, but this sensation was short-lived. I was soon concentrating on avoiding eye contact with the men in the green uniforms of the Schupo, the gray and black of the SS and the black of the Ukrainian militia. They were all there, and so were innumerable plainclothes Gestapo. There were even, God pity us, Jews posted by the Germans to point out brethren who were trying their luck at escape.

We walked behind Kolya through the large hall where tickets had once been sold from many booths, but now due to the war, from only two. Every step seemed like a mile; finally, Kolya reached the gate and presented our permits and tickets. First, the railroad clerk examined them; then, two uniformed guards did the same. The last inspection was made by a man in civilian dress, with a soft Italian hat and rimless eyeglasses. He looked at each document and, as Kolya pointed to each of us in turn, compared the photographs with our faces. There was no doubt. We were facing the Gestapo. Would we pass?

Kolya sounded foolish, saying, "Those people over there — they're my construction team for Organization Todt detail on the way to Dnepropetrovsk." Still, the inspectors at the gate must have taken him seriously, because soon, though nearly trampled by late arrivals, we found ourselves on the train platform. Within minutes, we were hanging from the steps of a rail car, and the conductor was blowing his whistle. The locomotive emitted a puff of steam and smoke — to us, at that point, it sounded like a sigh of hope. By the time we found seats, the train had left the station.

I stared out the window. There was a hollow feeling in the pit of my stomach, as we traveled past the Judenlager walls. My father was inside those walls, my mother and Abo and Wilo were with him. What, dear God, would happen to them? And then I knew. I would wait until I learned first hand about life in Dnepropetrovsk, until I acquired survival skills. Then I'd return and get them out. Somewhat prematurely, I swelled with hope. I felt I could save my family — all Jews — all mankind.

A German soldier sitting across from me, spat and said to his comrade, "There are saboteurs behind those walls. The pigs! thanks to the Führer, they're under police control."

We were crowded in by travelers dressed in civilian clothing like ourselves, officials on special assignment, and German businessmen, but, the car — and I imagine the entire train — was crowded with soldiers returning from leave to the front, eating their rations and cursing the fate that made them fight the "Russian swine" rather than the civilized western Allies. Now and then a soldier or civilian would direct a question or comment to me. I spoke German fluently but chose to answer in a lame mixture of German and Polish, hoping to fend off their curiosity. I noticed that other members of our group, though seated at random, did the same, as though we had all been instructed in how to act.

- 62 -

After a while, Kolya got up and went to the toilet. I did the same. I needed a few words with him, and some moral support.

"You're doing fine," Kolya assured me. "Just sit and pretend you're asleep. In an hour or so we'll reach Shepetovka," a town on the old Russian-Polish border. "There will be an inspection by the police and the Gestapo. Don't worry; I'll take care of the documents. After all," he said, smiling, "you're in my construction crew. I'm responsible for you."

He was as good as his word. In Shepetovka, the German MPs, accompanied by a plainclothes Gestapo man, boarded the train. Kolya showed them our papers and made some remarks. Before we knew it, our documents were stamped and counterstamped. The Germans seemed to respect anything that was printed. From that point on, I was considered by them as a legitimate Organization Todt man, a real Pole or even a Volksdeutcher. Foreseeing wide new horizons, I treated myself to a cup of ersatz coffee. I even mailed a card to my family — a futile act, considering that it would never arrive.

During the night, the train stopped at another checkpoint. The inspection here was more thorough than the one in Shepetovka, but, by now I was much more relaxed, to the point where I felt hungry. I helped myself to some warm soup, issued against a civilian ration card which Kolya had obtained with my travel permit.

The train rumbled slowly eastward. Unable to sleep, I looked out at the devastated countryside. Ragged Ukrainian children hung around the small stations, fighting over pieces of bread thrown by well-fed German soldiers. In more than one way, they were reminiscent of the hungry urchins in the Judenlager of Lvov.

A German civilian from Munich sat next to me. He explained that, as a member of the Nazi party in good standing, he had obtained a government contract to build industrial workers' barracks in the southwestern Ukraine. He wanted to impress me with his good feelings toward Poles, at the same time stressing that I looked more German than Polish. "You are the best proof of Nazi racial theory," he said at one point. "You're Volksdeutsch — I can see the German blood in your veins. Thank God and the Führer," he added, "your country is cleansing itself of the Jewish plague."

I realized then, that my new role would take me beyond a phony name and false papers: I had to start thinking and acting Polish or Volksdeutsch. "Yes, sir!" I responded. "Thank God and the Führer!" As I said it, I couldn't help thinking that I was lucky. Had my companion been a Pole or a Ukrainian, he wouldn't have been so easily deceived by my blond mustache and blue eyes.

At nine a.m., after a journey of twenty-four hours, the train pulled into the ruined Dnepropetrovsk terminal. Our proximity to the front line was clear from the throngs of soldiers and the freight trains loaded with military equipment. In all that confusion of people and machinery, one could make out the innumerable uniformed Ukrainian police and guess at the presence of the ubiquitous Gestapo plainclothesmen.

We followed Kolya, in haste to leave the station. It wasn't a safe place to linger. We walked several miles, past shells of houses and factories. We were in the outskirts of Dnepropetrovsk, an area that had been heavily industrialized under Soviet rule. Tens of thousands of factory workers had lived and worked in the ruined buildings we were now passing.

Kolya walked next to me for a few minutes, giving me our immediate plans. "You'll stay with a friend of mine, a fellow named Misza." He pointed to one of the men in our group, a man I had seen for the first time two nights before in the depot on Karna Street, in Lvov. I took a better look now. Even in those dangerous times, with the constant threat of violent death hanging over all of us, I felt cultural and social differences between us. A few years older than me, he had the appearance of someone who in normal times must have been a blue-collar worker, maybe a menial laborer. Husky, with square-cut features, he could easily be taken for a Ukrainian peasant.

We reached a small house at 85 Tretiaja Fabrika. Kolya knocked on the door, which bore the name Hryniewicz. It was opened by a middle-aged woman, a typical Ukrainian in a babushka. She smiled brightly.

"Ah! Pan Kolya!" she said. "It's been a long time!"

"Well over a month. I had to travel to Lvov, to collect Polish workers for my Organization Todt job. I'd like to ask you to help me with lodging for two of my men. What I have in mind is room and board — breakfast and dinner, and a sandwich they'll eat at work. You know that money is no problem. They'll pay you well, and you'll have two clean, quiet tenants."

The woman didn't need any persuading. She could use

the additional income. We parted from Kolya and followed our landlady into a pleasant room with two beds, a dresser, two shaky chairs and a colorful icon on the wall.

"Make yourselves at home," the woman said, or at least I assumed she said that. The Ukrainian that I had learned in Lvov and the Ukranian she spoke were two different tongues. Hers was a mixture of Russian and regular Ukranian, so by understanding some words, and by her gestures, I understood.

We had no sooner washed when she was back, announcing that lunch was ready. We sat at a large family table in the kitchen, a plate of scrambled eggs and bacon in front of each of us.

My background, of course, was strictly orthodox; never in my life had I been served non-kosher food. Until two days ago, I couldn't have imagined myself eating bacon. But the Talmudic rule of practicality, Pekuach Nefesh, came to mind. It means, among other things, that a Jew may act as a Gentile if it means the difference between life and death.

The eggs and bacon had an enticing aroma. I ate a piece of bread and swallowed a bit of bacon — it didn't taste bad. Misza ate like a starving wolf, and I began to follow his example, but, my stomach, reared in the orthodox tradition, didn't understand Talmudic reasoning. It remained kosher, and the result was painful. No sooner had I finished eating when I had to dash to the outhouse where I threw up the first non-kosher fare of my life.

There is no misery without some accompanying good. My roommate sympathized with my misadventure; he understood my stomach's culinary loyalties. We went out to the tiny orchard in back of the house, sat on a stump and swapped stories.

"Two years ago my parents were still alive," Misza said, "and I had six brothers and sisters. Today, I'm the only one left." He sighed deeply; sighs were a language of the Polish Jew during the Holocaust. "I have no education. I dropped out of school after the fifth grade, and I've worked as a stock clerk since."

"Do you think we'll make it here?"

"I don't know." Misza's simple face darkened. "I have a bad feeling about my own escape. But" — he flashed a smile — "why don't we take it as it comes? One day at a time."

Late that afternoon, our landlady's husband returned from work, as did her teenage daughter. They didn't seem a bit surprised to find two new faces at the dinner table. I supposed that when they looked at us, they simply saw some extra money for the family.

I could hardly sleep that night. Away from my family, uneasy in the midst of a tempest, I felt the full burden of loneliness. I wasn't even sure I would ever see Kolya again.

But Kolya came first thing in the morning to retrieve Misza and me. The landlord and his daughter had already left, and only Mrs. Hryniewicz, who had just cleared the breakfast table, was around. "Come on, boys! Hurry! Hurry!" Kolya called. "He who doesn't work, doesn't eat!" He carried if off so professionally that I wasn't sure it was intended only for our landlady; maybe we really were legitimate workers with regular jobs.

We left the house and walked for a while without talking. Finally I broke the silence.

"Are we going to a work site?"

"Not exactly," Kolya answered. "I owe you some clarification." Very briefly, he told us about our "Organization." A small group of militant young Zionists had arranged an underground railway to rescue as many Jews as possible. "Mostly the young ones," Kolya said, "so that once the Nazi plague ends we can develop a new type of Jew—fighters, not victims. They'll be strong and determined enough to win back the Land of Israel. It will be the only place on earth where anti-Semitism will be obsolete." Kolya belonged to the right-wing Zionist party Betar, as I had before the war.

"How does it work in Dnepropetrovsk?" I asked.

"We've rented a few apartments scattered around the outskirts. When I come to collect you in the morning, you'll go to one of those safe houses for the day. We'll tell the landlords there that you work on the night shift."

"It sounds good, but how long can it last?"

"I don't know. Maybe not too long. Once in a while we'll have to leave one apartment, and move into another."

"How dangerous is it to live here?"

"Dangerous compared to what?"

"Compared to the Judenlager in Lvov."

"Look. This isn't a picnic. It's dangerous, all right. The place is crawling with spies. There's the Gestapo, the SS, the Ukrainian police, and you can even run into General Vlasov's soldiers."

I knew about Vlasov. He was a Russian turncoat who,

with his army of half a million men, had defected to Hitler during the 1941 Nazi invasion. Many of his soldiers, Tartars, Kalmucks and Cossacks, would kill first and ask questions later.

"So," I said. "How do we manage?"

"Give yourself time. Soon you'll start seeing possibilities. The "Organization" can help you with false identity and work papers and all sorts of uniforms — Organization Todt, Wehrmacht, even SS. Incidentally, when you get an army uniform, you can also get a rifle, if you want, or a regulation pistol."

We stopped in front of a small house. Kolya knocked on the door, and a man opened it. I could hardly believe my eyes: the fellow had been a member of my Betar group before the war. We had a lot to talk about that day as we played "21" with five other men who were staying there.

From the others, I learned that not only Jews were concealed in Dnepropetrovsk. There were Poles as well, on the run from forced labor in Germany. But, some of them, we were told, had been assigned by the Nazis to find Polish Jews in hiding. We could trust no one!

At the end of the day, Misza and I, unshaven and dirty, returned to the Hryniewiczs to wash and share a meal. We made up stories of our first day on the job and told them at the table. We continued this routine until the end of the week, when we were able to spend all of Sunday at home: the first day off for this hard-working construction gang.

The conversation during our phony workdays always dealt with deportations, arrests, beatings and shootings.

Instead of feeling better away from the Judenlager, I developed the hunted-animal syndrome, a continuous anxiety, and a sensation of paranoia, where a friend was an enemy in disguise and isolation was the only imaginable security.

One day when I couldn't take it any longer, I described my feelings to Misza, "I'll go back to Lvov," I said, "to rescue my family." Even as I spoke, it seemed paradoxical. Unhappy in Dnepropetrovsk, I intended to drag my family to that miserable city. "Once we're together, everything will change," I hoped aloud. "I'll be able to find a real job instead of living in pretense."

To Misza, a trip to Lvov was suicide. "You're crazy," he said. "The first Ukrainian you run into will denounce you. It's a noble thought, but, my God! It's just plain stupid. I understand you, but I'd never dare try it myself.

"I don't think it's that impossible," I replied. "I've considered every detail, thought about it from different angles. It seems simple enough. No mystery. All you need is a set of documents with as many German stamps and signatures as possible, and, of course, you've got to have total self-assurance when you show them to the authorities. Don't laugh! All the Germans respect good paperwork with plenty of rubber stamps."

I came to believe just that. To the Germans, a rubber stamp was more real than an irreversible fact like circumcision. A counterfeit document presented with a smile might open a door. I decided to get false papers for every member of my family — signed and counter-stamped, not just by the regular authorities, but by the chief of the military district office in Dnepropetrovsk. They would seem even more authentic, and I would be on the way. I even invented an employer, Wiener Baugesellschaft — the Vienna Construction Company — with a post-office box for an address.

I approached Kolya with my plans. Strangely, he was as enthusiastic as I was. "There should be more like you," he told me. His support, however, was not without ulterior motives. He promised to help me with the masquerade on the condition that I not only bring my family, but help rescue some of his relatives and friends.

"But that will make twelve people, including you and me," I objected.

"True. We'll get six documents for you and six for me. We'll travel together, but once we get to Lvov, you'll go your way and I'll go mine until both groups are ready to escape. Then we'll travel together back to Dnepropetrovsk."

A period of intense preparations began. Kolya put me in touch with a Jewish printer and counterfeiter who lived in Dnepropetrovsk as a Pole. I supervised his production of furlough papers for twelve nonexistent construction workers.

After two weeks of meticulous work, I had all twelve sets of papers in my hands, with six names invented by Kolya and six by me. To make the scheme more plausible, we added "East Front Military Construction, Ost Einsatz" to the firm's name. That would entitle the bearer of the document to wear a German army uniform, or the white uniform of the Organization Todt. It was one more way to avoid contact with the Ukrainian or Polish police, to whom anyone in a uniform was German, and as such unstoppable.

When, in mid-May, Kolya furnished me with a green loden suit typical of a Bavarian burgher and, for a change of clothes, a Wehrmacht uniform — complete with loaded handgun — I felt a change come over me.

"I have the feeling an actor must have when he's on stage," I said.

"I'm a man wearing a mask."

"Well put. This whole town is a theater," Kolya said. "Everyone is in disguise; I don't know who's a friend and who's an enemy any more. Sometimes, when I look in the mirror, I back off in fear. More often than not, the reflection doesn't seem to be me. We're all wearing masks."

Dressed in my Bavarian outfit, a swastika on my lapel, a felt hat with a feather on my head and a briefcase with phony documents in my hand, I left the house with Misza. Now, wearing a neat suit, he came along as a lookout. We decided that he would get on the streetcar before I did. Once we reached the dreaded building from which the Nazi governor general ruled over the southern Ukraine, he would keep watch. Should I be arrested or shot, he'd leave his post and warn the others, since my capture might endanger many lives. Just in case, I carried the loaded gun in my pocket. Should things go sour, I thought, I'd kill one or two Germans and then kill myself. I arrived at the governor's mansion scared and elated.

As I passed two Ukrainian guards in front of the building, I raised my arm in the Nazi salute and said, "Heil Hitler!" They returned the salute without asking about my business. I went in and walked down a long corridor. I remember the hollow sound of my steps as they echoed through the corridor; my feet seemed somehow weighted with fear.

I stopped at a double door marked Gebietskommissar, provincial governor. I glanced at two Ukrainian policemen posted in front of it and asked in loud, clear German whether this was the main office. One of the sentries said, "Bitte!" and respectfully opened one of the doors for me.

An attractive young woman, presumably the governor's secretary, sat at the desk in the front room. She gave me a cursory look and asked me to sit down while she finished working on the day's mail. I waited hoping that the visit would end soon. Minutes dragged by as she dated each sheet of correspondence and put it aside. Finally, her work done, she looked up and smiled. She asked in German, "What can I do for you?"

I introduced myself. I was the Volksdeutsche Stanislaw Nowak, a foreman with the Wiener Baugesellschaft. I had come to have my furlough papers and those for my eleven-member crew stamped and certified for a two-week vacation.

"We're all from Lvov," I explained, "and we'll be spending the entire time there. After that we'll return to Dnepropetrovsk."

I displayed twelve sets of three-page documents — an Ausweis, which was a passport with a picture of the bearer; a company employment card; and a military permit bearing the dates of the furlough. The secretary collected all thirty-six sheets and advised me politely that she would take them to the military governor, for processing and signatures. It might take a while, she added. Excusing herself, she left through the same door I had used to enter her office.

I sat alone and uncomfortable. I noticed another door to the room, and decided it must lead to the governor's office. A large wall clock ticked — very slowly, it seemed. Five minutes passed, then ten. The only other noise was the occasional thump of boots out in the corridor. Whenever I heard steps, I would tense up. I could imagine Gestapo men and Ukrainian policemen bursting in. I could hear the governor shouting, "Arrest the impostor! Shoot the Jew!" Fifteen minutes went by, then twenty. I pushed my chair closer to the wall. From there, I could see both doors. I tucked my hand in my pocket and played with the gun. I was ready to shoot — them, myself, anybody. "God! Why does it take all this time!" I muttered.

Suddenly I heard the click of short steps in the corridor. I relaxed; it must be a woman. The door opened and the secretary came in, carrying a folder containing my documents. She smiled, sat down at her desk, and said, "I'm sorry it took so long. The governor was in a meeting. Now it will take me only a short time. I just have to fill in the names of your people over the signatures on our documents. I'd appreciate it, Mr. Nowak, if you'd spell out those Polish names for me — they're so outlandish."

I was still quite nervous, but the incongruity of the situation didn't escape me. I found the whole thing very droll. Here I was, escaped from the Judenlager of Lvov, bent over a good-looking Fraülein and spelling out for her all those names Kolya and I had invented. The humor increased when a Ukrainian policeman stepped in and

-74-

tried to leave a message with her. She dismissed him abruptly and, after he had gone, grinned conspiratorially at me. "He can't understand that I'm busy. That Russian swine."

It took her quite some time to type in all those names which seemed so exotic to her; I kept counting minutes. The typing ended, and I glanced hurriedly over the documents she handed back to me. Everything seemed to be in perfect order. The governor's signature was prominently displayed: F. A. Eisenblath. The papers were valid for a longer period than I needed, May 19 through June 23, 1943. Most important, there were permits for travel and border crossings between the southern Ukraine and Galicia, which meant Lvov and the territory around it.

I looked at the clock. Almost the entire morning had passed.

"I appreciate your help," I said to the secretary. "You may not have realized it, but we've spent several hours together. I probably kept you from your normal duties. I'm sorry."

"Oh!" She waved her hand. "If you're referring to those Russian pigs, don't worry. My name is Annaliese," she added, and suddenly I had the feeling that I was being flirted with.

"I'm Stanislaw Nowak." I blushed. "But you already know my name."

"You're going west. I envy you."

"Why?"

"It's boring here, and you can't get the necessities. Especially silk stockings. You can't find them in this godforsaken place."

"I don't want to seem too bold, but would it be all right if I brought you a pair from Lvov?"

She was delighted. "By all means! And when you do, we might have dinner together."

I remembered a humorous Russian novel about the early days of the Bolshevik revolution, about women who'd sleep with any man for a pair of silk stockings. My eyes roamed over the pretty young secretary.

"I think I'll bring you several pairs," I said, slipping the documents into my briefcase.

"Have a nice trip," she said. "Enjoy your furlough."

"Thank you, Fraülein Annaliese. I'll see you soon.

As I boarded the streetcar, so did Misza. He sat on the bench across from me. We didn't have the courage to speak to each other, but I could see the question in his eyes. I smiled.

Later, he joined me on the street. "So? How did it go?"

I gave him the details, and when we reached the house laid my prize on the table.

At that moment I realized something terrible had happened! I was two sets of documents short! The secretary had been so absorbed in telling me about the silk stockings that she'd scrambled the papers, and that could cost us dearly.

"What are you going to do?" Misza asked. "You can't go back. We've got to disappear."

I thought feverishly. Returning to Annaliese was the only solution. If I didn't go back, she might try to look me up in a nonexistent firm.

"There's no other way," I said. "I'll go back immediately." And I was off again, over his protests. When he saw that I was determined, he announced that he was changing his residence as of that moment.

As I stepped off the streetcar and entered the governor's building, I thought of Kolya's remark that Dnepropetrovsk was a city of masks. This time, I didn't even say, "Heil Hitler!" to the guards. I just walked into the office, as though I were an old friend of the governor.

And there she stood, my fair Annaliese, deep in conversation with two SS officers. As she saw me, she exclaimed happily, "There you are! Mein Fliegender Holländer! My flying Dutchman! You've saved me some work. I was about to telephone you that you'd forgotten two sets of documents, when these officers arrived to discuss something with me." Handing over the missing papers, she reminded me, "Remember the silk stockings."

I couldn't see Misza anywhere in the street. He wasn't in the apartment, either. Later, he came in cautiously after making sure I hadn't been followed. His reaction when he saw me, was uncharacteristic. He hugged me and all of a sudden, I saw that somber, husky laborer drop a tear.

The next morning, I met with Kolya and we set a date for our trip together. Later that day, bad tidings came. Kolya found that he was wanted by the Gestapo in Lvov. He could not travel with me.

"A relative of mine, Juzek, will be in charge of my part," he told me. "He's a good man, you can trust him."

I was in a quandary. Instead of a seasoned Kolya, I'd have to depend on another greenhorn like me. Practically speaking, it meant I would be on my own.

╫ ╫ ╫ ╫ ╫ ╫

CHAPTER

6

Return to Lvov

J UZEK WAS A SOPHISTICATED FELLOW whose education made up for his lack of experience. Following Kolya's suggestion, he and I agreed that we would share the rubber stamps that had been made by our counterfeiter. We didn't know whether the people we intended to save were still alive, and that created a problem. Should we need to replace the photos in the forged documents, stamps and signatures would have to be applied to the new pictures. So, if need be, we'd share the stamps and he could count on me to forge new signatures.

We also had to decide on our clothing for the trip. After studying the alternatives carefully, we decided that

Juzek would wear a Waffen SS uniform, while I would become a German army corporal. Misza, who owned two pairs of military boots, gave me one for good luck. And with that, five days after the governor had signed the furlough permits, we were on our way to Lvov.

We did something particularly daring at this point. We traveled together. As far as this went, there was only one agreed-on rule: whenever we had anything serious to discuss, we'd wait for the train to stop and talk outside. We also thought it would be safer to pretend to be asleep while the train was moving, to discourage attempts at conversation from unknown passengers.

Juzek turned out to be a good traveling companion. He was always composed, he was witty, and his easy laughter reassured me. I felt exhilarated. "A few more days," I repeated to myself, "and I'll be with my family." I refused to consider the possibility that my family was dead. I had a mandate to save them and a covenant with God. I was sure they were waiting for me and that I would reach them and save them.

I took off my military cap to wipe the sweat from my forehead. I could feel the bristly texture of my short cut hair. That alone set me apart from the Judenlager Jews, whose hair, by executive order, was cropped to the skin.

As the train left Fastow, a large town near Kiev, two Ukrainian soldiers from General Vlasov's turncoat army confronted us.

"How about a game of 21?" one of them said in terrible German. This presented a dilemma. To play meant to be in close contact with people who were used to sniffing out

Jews; not to play might arouse their hostility. We decided to play.

The Ukrainians sat on the bench facing ours, and one of them set down his valise, broad side up, as a card table.

"I've got fourteen," one of them mumbled in Ukrainian to the other.

"Don't ask for another card," his companion suggested. "Let those German suckers think you've got twenty-one."

They couldn't know that their "German suckers" understood every word they said. As the game went on, the two Vlasov men lost time after time, until a good deal of money had changed hands.

One of them persisted. "How about playing for our ration cards?" he asked.

That was something neither Juzek nor I wanted. "It's against the law," I snapped. "If you haven't got any more money, the game is over."

They had almost reached their destination in any case. Instead of bidding us farewell, they mumbled a few Russian epithets before getting off the train.

We resumed our "naps" as the train inched its way west. Soon we crossed the old border between Russia and Poland, and finally stopped in the town of Brody.

This time, I was calm when the German MPs and Gestapo agents boarded for document control. I handed over my papers to an MP, who passed them to a Gestapo man, who in turn rubber-stamped them and gave them back to me with a curt "Thank you!"

After the inspection, we went out to get rations of hot

soup and canned meat. I felt terrific. I flashed all six sets of papers I was carrying for my family and myself and received food for all. I congratulated myself on obtaining the best souvenirs of my travels as the man in charge of the mess hall stamped all the documents. The counterfeit papers had acquired a new validity: they now bore official proof of arrival from the southern Ukraine.

I crammed the precious food into my valise, and went out again to make final arrangements with Juzek.

"I don't think we should be seen together from now on," he said. "There are too many people who might recognize us. It'll have to be each man for himself, and may God help us."

We set the hour and the place for our next meeting: 8:30 p.m. on May 26, on the usually deserted Listopada Street near the Czwartakow labor camp.

As we parted, a throng of German soldiers boarded the train. Juzek was among them at one end of the car, and I was at the other end. Four hours after we left Brody, the train pulled into the main terminal in Lvov. Round one was over.

Now that I was in Lvov, repressed doubts surfaced. Was everyone in my family still alive? I had to make a few decisions immediately. I couldn't return to the Judenlager in a German uniform. What I needed very badly was the Jewish arm band, "W" patch and ghetto identity card that I had hidden in Ryzewskyj's kitchen. That meant I needed a Gentile to help me.

I thought of a man named Bogdan, a Ukrainian carpenter and one of Ryzewskyj's subcontractors. I had delivered building materials to him and learned a bit about him. He was a decent person who detested the Germans. He was also a businessman who had bartered with me on many occasions, trading food for clothing or jewelry. I was sure Bogdan would be the proper choice.

I grabbed the heavy valise with my civilian clothes and canned meats and, inconspicuous among the soldiers, struggled toward the streetcar stop.

A streetcar had just arrived, and in no time it was filled. While the back entrance was marked "For other Aryans," there was a sign on the front door stating, "Nur für Deutsche" — For Germans Only. A Ukrainian police-man stood there, one foot on the pavement, the other on the step, blocking access with his body. I shoved him aside, saying, "You stupid pig!" He stepped off, saluted, and pushed my valise in for me.

At that moment I was an Übermensch, a German Superman. With full awareness of my new role, I got off the streetcar a little before Bogdan's place, at Jagiellonska Street. I wanted to have the pleasure of crossing the Jezuicki Park, a patch of greenery in front of the University that was off-limits to Jews and dogs.

It was May 25, 1943, and a glorious morning. It took me a while to get to Bogdan's apartment, which was on Krasicki Street. Luck was with me so far, but I wondered if I would find him at home. I walked up to the second floor of his building and knocked on the door.

A man's voice asked, "Who's there?"

"A friend!" I kept knocking. "Open up!"

There he was, Bogdan, looking but not recognizing

me. I pushed him on the chest and he backed up a step. I came in and locked the door.

"Look!" I said hoarsely, taking the gun out of the holster and pointing it at him. "Take a good look. Can you tell who I am?"

He brought a hand to his mouth to muffle a gasp, of surprise and fear. "Izio?"

"You've got it!" I put my valise on the floor, pulled up a chair, turned it around, sat on it astride and rested my hand with the gun in it.

"What are you doing here? What do you want from me?" The man was panicky. In his eyes, every Nazi law had been broken: a Jew in an Aryan house, a Jew in German uniform, a Jew threatening him with a gun. "I've never hurt a Jew," he appealed.

"All right, Bogdan," I said cheerfully. "Not to worry. I know you're a good man who doesn't like the Nazis. I'm a member of a very strong partisan group, and I have a mission. Your place has been chosen as my temporary headquarters. There's just you and your wife, no children; that suits me fine."

"They'll shoot me if they discover that I took you in!"

"Correct! That's why you will make sure they don't find out. And, if anything happens to me, the partisans will kill you. You really don't have a choice."

Badly shaken, Bogdan was still standing. I pushed the gun back in the holster to put him at ease.

"That was the official part of my visit. Now let's talk as friends. Do you know anything about my family? Are they all right?"

"Yes. I saw them yesterday, in Ryzewskyj's courtyard. Your father and your brothers. There haven't been any deportations lately, so I suppose your mother must still be there, too."

I made myself at home. I took off my belt and laid it on the table; I hung my jacket on the back of the chair and unbuttoned my shirt.

The dining-room door opened, and Bogdan's wife came in, still in her nightgown. She stared at me, bewildered.

"The corporal is a friend of mine," Bogdan explained. "We've got business to discuss, so why don't you leave us alone?"

She disappeared obediently.

"You acted properly," I told my host. "Never discuss me with her. Remember, mum's the word."

"I won't talk. Please, just take care of your business and let us be."

"I'll do my best, but you've got to help me." I scribbled a note and handed it to him. "Take this to my mother in Ryzewskyj's kitchen. She'll give you my identity card, my arm band and the 'W' patch. As soon as I have them, I'll attend to my business. Oh, and before you go, tell your wife not to bother me. As far as she's concerned, I'm not here."

Bogdan made haste. The faster he helped me, the sooner he'd be rid of me.

I undressed, put on my civilian clothes, folded the uniform and slipped it in the suitcase under the cans of meat. I did the same with the belt but kept the gun in my pocket, just in case. I looked in the mirror. A slight, dark-blond man stood there, with a blond mustache. No longer a German soldier, I suddenly lost the Superman feeling and felt afraid and insecure. With the Jewish band back on my arm and the Kennkarte in my pocket, I knew I was going to feel devastated. "Courage!" I said to myself. "You're fighting for several lives. Don't let Bogdan see how you feel."

He was back within the hour.

"I saw your mother," he told me. "She's fine. Here's your I.D., the arm band, and the patch." He stared at me. "Strange! Without the uniform, you're the same old Izio."

"I'm not the same old Izio," I warned. "Make no mistake about it."

"On my way back, I picked up a horse and wagon at Ryzewskyj's stable," Bogdan added. "I thought you could use them. They're waiting in front of the house."

I left the apartment, to Bogdan' obvious but unexpressed relief. I dragged the valise downstairs and concealed it in the wagon under a pile of building supplies. I climbed up to the driver's seat and pulled on the reins, whispering to the horse, "Come on! Let's go to the kitchen!"

It was still early in the morning, and there were few people on the streets. I was stimulated by anticipation one moment, and overcome with apprehension the next. The wagon rolled slowly into the large courtyard formed by a building facing Kazimierzowska Street and another with its entrance on Wagowa Street. The kitchen was on the second floor of the Wagowa Street building.

I jumped off the wagon and looked cautiously around.

All at once, there they were — my parents. Forgetting where we were, they dashed toward me, hugging, kissing and crying. We went into the hall and stopped for a moment to control our emotions.

Someone had to remain calm. "Now, now," I said, patting mother on the shoulder. "This noise can be dangerous. Let's go upstairs, and I'll tell you everything as soon as we're alone."

Mother's co-workers noticed me and came running. The matter was getting out of hand. "Can we have some privacy for a minute?" I asked. Then and there, I was the center of everyone's attention.

Finally, we settled in a back corner and, as in the old days, returned to whispering. "Why did you come back?" mother asked anxiously. "It's bad here. We're reaching the end of the road."

"That's precisely why I came. I can get us all a fresh start. I'll get you out."

"You're a dreamer." She wiped away a tear. "Can't you hear the shooting?"

Recurring volleys could, indeed, be heard from a distance. "The Piaski, The Sand Mountain?" I asked.

She nodded sadly.

"They sealed off the Janowska camp, and they're trucking Jews out of there to Piaski. They're killing them."

This woman who had felt emotions for every human being, rejoiced in their joy and ached at their pain. Now she reflected only pain.

"I'll explain the whole thing when we're home," I said.

I still owed an explanation to the others who knew me.

They had figured out that I'd been away, but they didn't know where. Someone mentioned that I was believed to have been involved in the recent Warsaw Ghetto uprising. I shrugged and said only, "I'll tell you one of these days." No one could be trusted; even a friend or a relative could turn one in.

From the kitchen, I went to Ryzewskyj's offices. The first person I ran into was Baranskyj, the engineer and manager and the man who had once helped me rescue my father.

"What are you doing here?" he asked.

"I was sick with typhus. Very sick. I'm better now, I'm ready to work."

Even to me the story sounded phony. I looked healthier than ever, well-fed and tanned, and certainly not a typhus patient.

In any event, Baranskyj couldn't care less. He gave me an assignment for the day, and I left to make his deliveries.

Some fellow workers stopped me and asked questions. "I was with the partisans," I said this time, and instantly regretted it. Well, what was done was done.

After the day's work, I returned to the kitchen for some soup. That was when I saw my brothers. Abo looked haggard and strained; Wilo looked even younger than his age, thin and pale. Impulsively, we hugged and then quickly restrained ourselves. Many eyes might see us.

As Ryzewskyj's Jewish labor detail marched back to the Judenlager, grim memories returned. I started at the wall and the guards, and my heart skipped a beat in memory of the flogging. The decaying houses, the starving people lying on the street corners waiting to die — it was a vision from Dante's Hell. One month on the Dneper River had almost made me forget the bleakness of the ghetto. "I'll get them out," I promised myself.

At home, we exchanged news. "They're liquidating the work details," father said. "Many of your friends, many of your relatives, are dead."

"Soon it'll be our turn," mother sighed.

I pounded on the table. "That's why I'm here! To get you out!"

"You're talking nonsense," mother replied.

"Here, I've got the papers!" I laid the documents in front of them. "For father; for Abo; for Wilo; even for Shmuel Panzer and Shia Guthstein!" The last two were our cousins. "I couldn't get documents for you, mother."

The ensuing silence was painful. As we looked into each other's eyes, I knew she understood the problem. What kind of worker could she pretend to be? She was in her fifties, and while her face still showed signs of beauty, it also showed the deep lines that came from raising five children and from her current suffering.

"You've got to trust me," I continued. "It's much easier for men. They'll travel as Organization Todt workers, in white uniforms and all. I'll tell them Wilo's an apprentice. But the only women working near the front lines are young, mostly clerks and secretaries. You can't come with us, but I'll be back for you. One step at a time. I swear to you."

Mother pondered the situation. "What if they should

catch you? Our entire family would be wiped out. Maybe you should only take two men this time. Maybe Abo and a cousin?"

"And what about the Piaski? We might survive if we try to escape; staying here is like suicide. Anyway, I've got business to attend to. I'll be back soon. Talk it over."

There was one more item on my agenda. I wanted to see Nesia again. I had asked about her before, and had been told she was alive and living in one of the few nice buildings remaining in the Judenlager.

At the outbreak of war, Nesia's family, originally from a small town in eastern Poland, sought shelter in Lvov, but in 1940 the Russians deported her parents and brothers to Siberia. She managed to remain in the city, staying with an aunt.

With the arrival of the Nazis, she found employment with the Judenrat, the Jewish Council of Elders, and worked there until its liquidation during the action of September 1942. After that, I lost contact with her. There were rumors that she had found work in the labor camp Czwartakow, in the northern section of the city. It was said that her detail was escorted to and from the camp every day by Jewish policemen. I was also told that a man named Altman, an officer of the Jewish Police and a Gestapo collaborator, had fallen in love with her. Altman's job was to discover Jews in hiding, he also had the opportunity to protect Nesia and must have saved her life on several occasions when other young women were being deported.

That must have been the reason she had married him.

I reached the building where Jewish Police collaborators had their apartments, and where some of the other employees of the Germans lived. Altman's name was on a door on the first floor. I knocked, and the door opened immediately. Nesia stood there, pretty as before, glad to see me and terribly sad at the same time.

She invited me in. I found myself in the kitchen. "How have you been?" I asked. It was an unnecessary question, but etiquette required it.

"I'm all right. How did you find me?"

"Somebody told me where you were. Nesia, I have very little time and I'd better get to the point immediately. I want you to leave the city with me. I think I can save your life."

"Shhh!" She brought a finger to her lips. "Not so loud. My mother-in-law is in the other room. What do you mean? How can you save my life?"

I spoke in a rush of words. I told her about Dnepropetrovsk, about the false documents, how she could travel as a Polish secretary, and how she could save her life and restore her dignity.

She was confused and speechless. The door opened abruptly, and a man came in wearing the uniform of a Jewish Service officer. I knew this must be Altman.

"Who's this?" he asked Nesia. "What does he want?"

"I'm a friend of Nesia," I explained, seeing that she was unable to speak. "We knew each other when we were in school."

"You're intruding, and I want you out!" he shouted. I blushed angrily. "Whoever I am," I yelled back, "I don't have any Jewish lives on my conscience. I don't sell lives to the Germans!"

"None of your damn business what I do! You have to step over bodies if you want to stay alive. Get out before I arrest you."

Both of us were fuming. Altman's mother looked in from the next room and watched us. Nesia cried.

"All right, I'll go." I said to Nesia. I realized Altman could destroy me and my family. "It was nice to see you again."

I left quickly and rushed home. I was upset, and my face was flushed as my mother opened the door for me.

"What happened, Izio?" I couldn't hide my unhappiness, and described the events of the past hour. She broke into tears. "God help us! Don't you see what you've done? You've jeopardized us all!" Crying, and wringing her hands in despair, she was a picture of doom. I felt horrible; there was nothing I could say.

The family talked until late into the night. The conclusion seemed inevitable: everyone would come with me, except mother. She would stay in the ghetto, and one day in the near future I would come back for her. In the meantime, if she faced any emergency, she would seek shelter with the Prachtels.

Going to work the next morning, I was afraid that my tan would attract Grzymek's attention. I bent down and stayed inside the group. At the gate, in the daily inspection, the Nazis picked up an old man from another work group. He would be executed. With a sigh, we left the Judenlager glad we were spared.

I managed to arrange my work so that I could spend several hours alone with my father and brothers. I had to teach them how to act on the outside, how to act non-

Jewish. It was a speed course in Aryanism. The topics included the German salute, the importance of speaking as little German as possible, and avoiding looking guilty when questioned.

Our biggest problem was fear. We had been ground down so far that a German could easily sense it. "Jewish eyes are constantly filled with fear," I tried to impress on them. "Jews don't look different from Poles or Ukrainians. There's no particular smell in your body that will betray you. It is that eternal terror in your eyes that marks you. Get rid of it!"

I had experienced fear. I knew that documents, Aryan names and uniforms meant nothing without a bearing of boldness and arrogance.

Each of them had to learn his new Polish name. Father became Wladyslaw Tyszkiewicz; Abo, Piotr Siminski; and Wilo, Stasio Grabowski. As of now, we would address each other using these names. We had to think of ourselves as strangers, brought together by chance.

I later located Shmuel, who worked in a warehouse, and gave him his Polish documents. I wasn't able to track down the other cousin, Shia, and his papers remained with me for the time being.

When the workday was over, I was faced with a major decision: whether to go to the Judenlager for the night or find shelter outside. It seemed to me that I had become too conspicuous to be seen again at the gate to the Judenlager. I didn't want to go to Bogdan, because he lived far away and an unfriendly eye might spot me in the streets. I picked a third option.

There was a streetcar operator I knew, a man named

Stefanskyj. He lived one floor above Ryzewskyj. I figured that a lion's den might offer the best protection to a stray lamb. And it was a lion's den: the Ukrainian mayor of the city lived in the same building, and right across the street there was the Ukrainian police precinct and a Gestapo substation.

As the detail gathered for dinner in the communal kitchen, I emptied my suitcase. I distributed almost all the canned meat to my parents and brothers, to use as means of exchange. I concealed my uniform, belt and boots in a bag, which I then placed in the valise. After that, my family returned to the Judenlager, while I sneaked into Ryzewskyj's building.

It was an imposing structure with two canopied entrances and three stairwells. I took the back stairs, and climbed cautiously to the third floor. Then came the moment of truth. I took the gun out and knocked.

Stefanskyj opened without asking who his visitor was. He stood in the door way staring at me and the gun.

I stepped inside and he backed away. I shut the door.

"Why do you want to shoot me?" he stammered. "I've never hurt you or any other Jew."

"Where's your wife?" I asked calmly.

"She's away. Visiting with her parents, in a village near here."

"When will she be back?"

"In a week."

"Step into the bedroom." I had to be sure he wasn't lying. I followed him in. The room was empty. I sat on the bed and played with the gun.

"Listen carefully. I've got something to tell you. Just

follow my instructions and I won't hurt you. See? I'm putting the gun away." As I put it on the bed next to me, I could see Stefanskyj relax a little.

"I'll listen," he said.

"I'm a messenger for the resistance. Your place has been chosen because the partisans know you don't like the Nazis. I'll use it as a base for my operations. Don't worry—it won't take more than a week at most. Just give me a set of keys, and you can go about your own business. Only don't say a word about me to anyone. Not even to your wife!"

He stared at me dumbfounded as I put on my Wehrmacht uniform. "I'm on a dangerous mission," I added. "We're desperate people."

"Please!" Stefanskyj begged. "Keep the other partisans away! The Germans will kill me if I am found out."

"I'll do what I can to make your life easier. Just remember: don't say anything!"

After that, we were somewhat more friendly. He fixed a light dinner, and we shared a can of my meat. It was getting late by now, and I had an appointment with Juzek at 8:30. Stefanskyj offered a toast. "One for the road!" We emptied the glasses, and I left.

I took two streetcars to get to Listopada Street. It was dark when I arrived, and no one was in sight. I realized with a start that Rozia lived in hiding in one of the buildings nearby. I had to suppress an urge to see her, and reason prevailed. To knock on the Prachtels' door would be dangerous for everybody.

Waiting alone in the street, I felt great anxiety. Was this the right place? If it was, where was Juzek? Maybe something had happened to him. I touched my gun and felt a little more secure.

After a twenty-minute wait, I was about to leave when suddenly, Juzek materialized.

"Everything's fine," he reported. "I contacted all five people. Each of them lives in the Aryan Quarter. I shouldn't have any problem getting them out."

Juzek had five sets of documents to use, the sixth was his own.

"I'm still looking for my cousin Shia," I said. "I think we'd better meet tomorrow evening. If I don't find him by then, I'll transfer the papers to someone else. One way or another, we should leave the day after tomorrow."

With that, we parted.

I stopped at the main railroad station and arranged return-trip tickets and permits for two days later. Then I returned to Stefanskyj's. The lights in his apartment were on causing me to lose some of my composure. I thought that perhaps he had denounced me. I unholstered the gun and tiptoed up the dark stairs.

Stefanskyj was in his kitchen, wearing only his pants. "Will you have a glass of tea with me?" he offered. As we sipped the tea, he asked a lot of questions about my mission. I evaded them, switching the subject to his work and to politics. At length, feigning fatigue, I excused myself and went to bed. But I slept very little that night. I felt under tremendous stress.

I got up from bed as soon as Stefanskyj left for work, stood at the window and looked into the courtyard. The whole situation was ironic. On the floor below, Ryzewskyj was probably still asleep. On the same floor, across the yard, his brother-in-law, the mayor of Lvov, might be having his morning coffee. And here I was, a Volksdeutscher or a Jew, with one of the most crucial days of my life ahead of me.

I put on my civilian suit, my arm band and the "W" patch, and went down to the courtyard, where Ryzewskyj's Jewish work detail was forming. It might have been my imagination, but I felt that my co-workers were eyeing me suspiciously. Some of them made oblique remarks about the partisans and offered their services. One, a man named Schneider who had a bad leg, limped toward me.

"I have a proposition for you," he whispered. "I've got gold coins- — lots of them. I'll give you half if you help me escape."

"I'm not interested," I said. I didn't like Schneider. "I'll give you all I have," he insisted. "Just get me out of here. Me and my wife."

"I don't believe you have much money. The only person with a lot of gold coins was that roofing contractor, Katz. But someone broke into his basement and stole two large pots of coins — they said it was Satz, the head plumber."

"It wasn't Satz. It was me!" Schneider disgusted me. In any case, I had come back to save my family. The gold coins would have to wait.

I suggested to my father and brothers that they go to the Jewish doctor and report in sick. I needed to talk to them, and the tiny clinic seemed to be the only place with some degree of privacy.

"We'll be leaving tomorrow," I told them. "Keep rehearsing, and wait until you hear from me."

I had a lot to do. I still hadn't contacted Shia. I had to discuss the uniforms with Shmuel. He was in charge of the warehouse, and I had to tell him that we were almost ready to go.

As I was crossing the courtyard, I was told Ryzewskyj wanted me. He was waiting in his office, his freckly, round face was purple with anger.

"You Jew bastard!" he yelled. "What's going on? I heard rumors that you're up to something. Look at yourself—you haven't got typhus! I'll tell you what you are. You're a goner. I won't turn you in to the Gestapo just yet, but only because I knew you before the war. I'm giving you two days to turn over your patch and your work papers."

Without those, a person was as good as dead. I tried to sooth Ryzewskyj, telling him that the rumors were lies and begging for a reprieve. Nothing helped. A Ukrainian big shot, he had his life well planned and wouldn't let me spoil it for him. My activities might jeopardize his firm's standing with the Gestapo.

There was no question now that I had to hurry. Not mentioning the incident in the office to my family, to spare them the worry, I rushed in my wagon to Shmuel's warehouse. There, Jewish laborers were sorting second hand civilian and military clothing and a variety of other items for the Germans. Shmuel's family had run a similar business before the war, and at least one of his present workers, Mundzio, had been in his employ for years. I had a brainstorm: since Mundzio was in charge of the company's horse and wagon, he could take my family and Shmuel to the train.

I spent some time with Shmuel, coaching him in the basics of acting like an Aryan. Then I gave him his documents and told him the time of departure and the route the wagon should take. I also gave him my old address in Dnepropetrovsk, and described the main features of the trip. This was just in case something should happen or if he should be forced to travel alone.

I finally came to the main point. "My people and you will need German uniforms. Which ones would you recommend?"

"I'm for the white O.T. ones. People of all ages wear them."

My mood had improved by the time I left the warehouse. Everything had been arranged. My father and brothers would get their uniforms; the warehouse had an abundance of them. And Mundzio would give my family a lift to the terminal.

Once again, I went to look for Shia. I visited several job sites, but could not find him. Eventually I gave up.

At the end of the day, I returned to the company kitchen. I had to make final arrangements with my family. "Tonight," I said, "you'll go to the Judenlager. Tomorrow morning, you'll report to work as usual, except that you'll have to bring small bundles with your personal necessities. When you see Mundzio's wagon in the courtyard sneak over to it, but remember, one at a time. He'll take you to Shmuel's warehouse first. You'll get your O.T. uniforms there. Now, pay attention! You'll undress. Put on the O.T. uniforms; then wear your civilian clothes on top of them.

"Mundzio will take you to the railroad station. On the way, his wagon will cross Pierackiego Street. There are high wooden fences on either side; you'll take off your civilian clothes there. Later, Mundzio will burn those clothes, your arm bands and your I.D. cards. I expect you to be at the station between eight and half past eight."

Then, unsure of myself, I offered my mother a chance to come with us. "Cut your hair short, put on a young girl's dress, and I'll try to smuggle you out as a secretary."

"I'm grateful," she said. "But the idea is crazy. Nobody in his right mind would take me for a young woman. I won't jeopardize your lives. Everything is in the hands of the Eternal. If I'm meant to live, I'll live."

"Then promise me that if things get worse, you'll hide with the Prachtels. Since Judge Prachtel was taken to Russia and may have been killed there, she is all alone, and ready to protect you and Rozia if you ask her to do so."

"I promise." she said.

"And I promise to come back. I'll return especially for you, and I'll take you with me."

We embraced and gave each other a goodbye kiss. It was our last. I never saw my mother again.

╫ ╫ ╫ ╫ ╫ ╫

CHAPTER

7

———

Exodus

WITH THE HORSE AND WAGON safe in Ryzewskyj's stable, I climbed the steps to Stefanskyj's apartment, changed into my Wehrmacht uniform and went to meet Juzek.

He was wearing an SS uniform. I found him tense, his usual good humor gone, and asked what was troubling him.

He shook his head. "Nothing in particular. It's just the awful bleakness here, and all the killing up there on Piaski. This is no way to live. When are you planning to leave?"

"Tomorrow morning."

"I'm not quite ready. It'll take me two more days. I've found one more friend I'd like to take with me, if I can have the papers."

Shia's documents were still unclaimed. "Here," I said, "you can have my cousin's set. I can't find him. You'll just have to change the photograph."

Juzek thanked me. We parted and went our own ways. This was the last time we saw each other.

Back at Stefanskyj's, I burned my Jewish I.D. and the arm band. Lying in bed that night, I understood the full meaning of the phrase "burning one's bridges." This was the end of my youth, and the start of a new life — would it be a short one?

In the morning, I repeated the previous day's pattern. I got up after Stefanskyj left for work. I ate a leisurely breakfast, read the local Ukrainian paper to learn if any American ships had been sunk by U-boats, and even laughed over a reference to President Roosevelt as "that Jew Rosenfelt."

I got to the railroad station half an hour early. Soldiers were rushing about, and the security was heavy. At the gate to the tracks, next to the ticket-verification clerk, stood several German MPs and two plainclothes Gestapo agents. There were no Ukrainian policemen in sight — a good omen. No one could match them at ferreting out Jews in hiding.

With departure time approaching I became more nervous. I left the lobby and waited outside. Twenty minutes later, I began to worry. Where were they! The train had to be boarded in the next few minutes, or we would be left behind. Where was my family?

At last there they were, all of them, except Shmuel. Abo was there with Wilo, looking like a Boy Scout with his spare shoes hanging from his rucksack. Father resembled an old-time Austro-Hungarian soldier in his white uniform, his face clean-shaven except for a short mustache. His get up gave him the necessary non-Jewish look.

I asked Wilo to put his shoes inside his pack, and we entered the lobby. Our time was running out, so we hurried to the gate and joined another group of latecomers, several German soldiers. Father and brothers were behind me in line. I approached the MPs and gave one of them the pile of documents and tickets, explaining that we were Organization Todt men returning to the Ost Einsatz, the eastern front. The MP glanced at the photos, compared them to our faces, returned the papers to me and passed the tickets to the clerk. A minute later we were on the train, which, following German custom, departed exactly on time.

We all sat in the same section of the car, breaking our rule for trying to remain inconspicuous. The others in the car, with the exception of two civilians, were Wehrmacht men, who would face their most serious challenge — the Russian front, once again.

I found the ride past the Judenlager wall quite painful. My mother was alone behind that wall! I prayed silently but fervently for her survival.

The four of us did our best pretending to be asleep. I listened to a German civilian next to me as he told some soldiers the short, tragic history of the uprising in the Warsaw Ghetto. "The Jewish pigs, with help from the Polish bastards murdered our innocent comrades from the SS," he said. At that point, I felt his gaze piercing me. I stared at him for a second and nodded my agreement. The man then confronted me directly.

"And who are all you people in white?"

"O.T. workers from Poland," I said with indifference. "A few of my construction team, returning from a furlough."

"Even the child?"

I chuckled. "Stasio is an excellent painter's apprentice. He's almost fifteen — he looks young for his age."

The man brooded for a moment.

"Yes, I see, even boys are fighting for us on the front."

"Well, our work is near the front line. It's part of the effort. Besides, we're all part of the Deutches Volk."

"How nice! I myself have a construction company in Cologne. Of course, as a party member in good standing, I've gotten a couple of good military contracts." He snorted with satisfaction, and then sat back, and went to sleep.

We napped intermittently, and the train finally reached the old Polish-Russian border. I knew how father and Abo must be feeling — very uncomfortable, to say the least. But, remembering my warnings, they were trying not to let it show, and not even I could see their fear. Wilo was still a child, yet he showed no fright outwardly. I waved the pile of papers under the nose of one of the border MPs; as usual, he passed them over to the Gestapo agent. Soon they were stamped and returned with a polite "Danke schön!"

The train pulled out of the border stop an hour later. Three more members of my family had received their "Aryan baptism."

At the next stop, in the Russian Ukraine, free food was being distributed at a large railroad commissary for traveling Germans in uniform. We joined the line of German soldiers and other persons with special travelling papers. Later we had a whispered, private conversation.

Father was making progress with his disguise. His jacket collar up, an extinguished cigarette butt in the corner of his mouth, he'd turn to me now and then and mumble. "So, Mr. Nowak? So how are things?" A Yiddish-speaking Hasid who could hardly boast of fluency in Polish, he tried to limit himself to those two Polish phrases for the duration of the trip.

After eating our fill of thick soup and bread, we returned to the train. Night had come, and with it darkness, the one real friend of a man on the run. The Judenlager syndrome — constant fright — was easing, and we were ready for some real sleep, at last.

It was early in the morning when the train stopped again. When I awoke, I found that father, Abo and Wilo had gone out on their own to get breakfast. They had taken my I.D. card, and when I joined them, Abo gave me the meal he'd obtained for me. Going out alone was a tremendous achievement for them.

After a good night's sleep and a large breakfast, the group's spirits were high. Yesterday seemed a long time ago, and my father and brothers seemed to have distanced themselves from the Judenlager somewhat. It was the elation of beginners, and it was up to me to put things in perspective. "I hear that we'll get to Dnepropetrovsk on time," I said. "At 9 a.m. sharp. We'd better get together near the toilet for a little chat."

I briefed them on our situation. "The Dnepropetrovsk terminal is heavily guarded like the one in Lvov. We'll leave as quickly as possible. If any of you are asked to show your documents, remember that I'm in charge of the group. To make things easier, we'll mix into a crowd of people, and try to avoid being spotted."

I lit a cigarette and tried to smoke, but ended up coughing, so I doused it. I was feeling the heavy weight of responsibility for the family. The trick was not to linger at the terminal, but to cross the waiting room and get onto the street as quickly as possible.

As the train pulled into the station, I looked out a window to try to gauge the risks. When I signalled the group, they filed behind me and into a large group of German soldiers.

At the control point, I once again explained that I was an O.T. foreman returning from furlough. The MP waved us through.

"Everybody follow me to the Sammelplatz!" I yelled in German, as though we actually had an assembly point. We all looked straight ahead, trying to avoid eye contact with strangers, and rushed out. Within minutes, we turned into a side street where we could no longer be seen from the station; I paired up with father, and Abo followed with Wilo. We walked for a long time, never pausing, through the outskirts of the city, past the old steelworkers' quarters to Tretiaja Fabrika number 85.

I knocked, and Mrs. Hryniewicz opened the door.

"Ah, Mr. Nowak!" she exclaimed. "How nice to see you!"

As we entered, she stared at Abo and remarked. "This

young man looks very much like you, Mr. Nowak. Is he your brother?"

Instead of answering, I introduced everyone by alias and repeated our cover story.

"What we need now," I said, "is a nice room. Would you have one for us?"

"You know the room I have. You stayed there with your friend Misza. He moved out some time ago. The room is available — the problem is that there are only two beds, and there are four of you."

"We're simple people. We'll double up. Of course, we'll take two meals a day, as I did before."

Mrs. Hryniewicz led us into the bedroom. "Wash" she said as she headed for the kitchen. "I'll call you when breakfast is ready."

The room seemed like home to me. "What do you think?" I asked the others.

"I think that I'm exhausted," replied father. It had been a long, traumatic day for him. The years in the ghetto and Judenlager had drained his endurance. Still dressed, he fell onto the bed and was soon fast asleep.

Abo, Wilo and I went out to wash while the landlady scrambled some eggs. As we re-entered the bedroom, we could hear father talking in his sleep. Not a worrysome thing as such, but here it made us shudder. He was calling to our mother in Yiddish!

I shook him violently by the shoulder and said, "Papa be careful! You'll get us all killed!"

Before breakfast, we went to the orchard behind the house for another of my briefings. "I have to stress that no one should be able to identify us as a family, "We're strangers to each other, the only language we are to speak, even among ourselves, is Polish. Occasionally we can speak German. Remember: no fear in your eyes; no family ties; not one Yiddish word!"

I forgot to mention the fourth rule — non-kosher food must be consumed. As we took seats at the kitchen table, Mrs. Hryniewicz brought out a huge platter of eggs and bacon, bread, butter, milk and ersatz coffee. Three of us helped ourselves eagerly. Father declined his portion. "I'm not hungry," he explained. "Maybe I'll just have some bread and butter with coffee."

We understood his feelings, but I wondered how long he could keep up a fast and whether we should allow him to follow his deep religious feelings. He might starve himself to death.

I excused myself after breakfast, saying I was going to see Misza for the latest news of Dnepropetrovsk.

The tidings were almost catastrophic. I had to knock on the door for a long time before Misza decided to answer. "Use the back door!" he said in a loud whisper, reminiscent of the old days in the Judenlager.

Misza was in a bad way. He sat down and buried his face in his hands. Then he raised his head. "Tell me about the Judenlager. How is it there? Did you get anyone out?"

"I brought my father and two brothers, but my mother and cousins are still there. Most people are just waiting to die! Frequently you hear shooting in Piaski. People are being deported constantly, or talking about deportation."

"That is enough. Now, I'll tell you about Dnepropetrovsk. The plague has reached us here. A few days after you left, there was a house-to-house search for Jews. They shot people on the spot, or took them to Gestapo headquarters and tortued them. In our old neighborhood, near the Hryniewiczs, the Gestapo knew which houses to search — some of the people they arrested must have informed."

"I was just lucky. But I'm going crazy; it's as bad as the Judenlager. I stay at home all day — sometimes I stick my head out at night and visit a friend. You're the only one who knows my address, by the way. I wouldn't trust anybody else. My landlady is a good woman, but give her a little time. How smart does she have to be to figure out I'm not Polish? If I were you, I'd move immediately. Four of you can't stay hidden for very long."

I was stunned. After all I had done to get my family out of Lvov, we had landed in the midst of yet another fire storm. I had expected problems, but not this severe and not this soon. All I could think of to say to Misza was, "So, this means we won't be seeing each other very often. We'll meet, only in emergencies."

"I suppose so. But still, I would like to meet your family, just once."

"Stop by later in the evening. Come in from the garden side, otherwise the landlady or her family might see you."

Finding another room was imperative. I took a local newspaper from Misza, looked in the "Rooms for Rent" ads and chose an address in the Pasiolok Frunze section, a hamlet just outside of town — 9 Czernomorskaja Street. I'd answer the ad the next day.

Back at home, I found father and my brothers relaxing in the orchard. I didn't have the heart to tell them what I'd heard, so I said simply, "Misza will drop by at eight." Then, as if it were an afterthought, I added, "I understand they've picked up a few Jews in this neighborhood. Just for security's sake, I think we should move to another place. So please don't leave the room until I've found a new one."

After that the conversation turned to mother. "I feel guilty," father said. "I shouldn't have left your mother alone." Then, staring at me, he asked, "When will you be able to get her out?" What could I say? I changed the subject, and speculated as to why Shmuel hadn't come with us.

We ate dinner early, at my request; I wanted to avoid sitting at the table with Mrs. Hryniewicz's husband and daughter, who would be home from work soon. We had bread, potatoes, a tiny amount of meat, some fruit and a fermented Russian drink called kwas. A bad dinner to begin with, it was even worse for father, who, out of respect for the Jewish dietary law, ate only the fruit and bread and drank some kwas. As we were finishing, the landlord and his daughter arrived. This time, it seemed to me that Mr. Hryniewicz wasn't at all happy to find new faces in his house. He asked merely if everyone worked with me, then left to wash his hands.

Father looked exhausted. Fifty-five years old, though his papers said sixty-five, and very frail, he wasn't used to this kind of life, and our mother's fate was constantly on his mind. The uncertainty was crushing. He went back to our room, prayed silently, and fell asleep.

I decided to have a talk with Abo and Wilo. Sitting

under the fruit trees behind the house, surrounded by the scent of flowers, I gave them the bad news. They agreed that we had to move, without telling father the full extent of the danger.

Misza arrived, hugging us as though we were all brothers. Father joined us, refreshed by his nap, and we talked mostly of the past, carefully avoiding the present and the future. Misza soon realized that father hadn't been told about the situation in Dnepropetrovsk. We talked a little more, and then he left. I accompanied him down the street and told him we'd be moving shortly.

In the morning, I got up as soon as the landlord and his daughter left the house and went to the kitchen. The landlady pumped me with questions about the others; I told her I'd be going to the plant to find out about our new work site. I added that it would probably be far away, and that travel might be involved. I also indicated that our group still had a few vacation days left.

Taking a streetcar to Pasiolok Frunze, I searched out the building and the rental I'd seen advertised, a two-story structure housing several families. I knocked at apartment one, on the left side of the front hall, introduced myself to the landlady and showed her the ad.

"I need a room for myself and three others. Two of them work with me. The third is the father of a friend of mine who works near the front line."

"I have a room," she said, "but it's got only two beds. I could add a cot, but I definitely can't give you four beds."

"That's all right. One of them is young. We can double up."

"And something else. I can't offer you board. My husband and I both work. He works during the day, and I'm working the night shift. But you're welcome to use the kitchen; you can buy food in the market nearby."

"That's fine, I'll pay you a month's rent in advance now, and we'll move in this evening." I liked the neighborhood. It was a working-class quarter, quite unlike the area of single-family houses where we were staying.

When I returned, I found the rest of the family quite worried by my long absence. "It's all right," I said cheerfully, "we're moving out tonight. Start packing."

We had dinner with Mr. and Mrs. Hryniewicz and their daughter. As the meal ended, I said, "I've got some news for you." I looked straight at Mrs. Hryniewicz. "It's not very pleasant." She was all ears; everyone in German-occupied territory was alert for bad news.

"It's about the four of us. We love staying with you, but — well, you know what it's like. Our new work site is a couple of hours away, and we'll have to move to a place nearer to it. In fact, I've already found a room. We'll be leaving tonight. I'm sorry."

"Wait a minute!" the landlady said. "We have an agreement!" Obviously, she had been counting on the rent money. I smiled at her. "I've thought this over. A deal is a deal. We took your room for a month; we paid you rent for a month. So enjoy it! The money's yours."

I could see the anxiety leave her face. If she'd had any doubts about us, my gesture must have eliminated them. It seemed like old Polish generosity.

With our bundles packed, we sat one last time in the

orchard, waiting for darkness. No one spoke for a while. Then, father reopened the painful subject.

"I'm very sorry that I came with you. I should have stayed with your mother and waited for you to get both of us out together. If that was to be God's will. At least we would have been together." He was crying.

Tears rose in my own eyes. "Papa!" I said. "Do I have to keep telling you how much I wanted to take her with us? It just wasn't possible! Just as soon as I can get my hands on the right documents, I'll go back to Lvov and bring her here. I swear!"

"Do you really think you'll go back? And risk your life? I shudder when I think I might lose both you and your mother."

We fell into each other's arms, sobbing.

Later, we walked to our new room, first through the empty streets of our old neighborhood and then through an unfamiliar section on the outskirts of the city. The only sign of life was the occasional dog barking in the darkness. Should anyone have noticed us, we would have seemed suspicious, four figures with little backpacks, sneaking along. We had chosen not to risk public transportation, this made things more difficult for father.

"We're getting near," I said when we were within a couple of blocks of our new place. "Wait around the corner for about five minutes. I'll go inside to make sure everything's in order. If you don't see me and there aren't any suspicious noises, you can follow."

I picked up father's pack and went to the house. The landlady's husband was inside, waiting for the new tenants.

"Where are the others?" he inquired. His wife must

have told him about us, including the advance payment, because he was quite friendly. I put the knapsack down and said, "They should be here in a minute. I think I'll wait for them right here."

A couple of minutes later, there was a knock on the door and the rest of my family filled the small hall.

"I'll take you to your room," the landlord offered.

"I know where it is," I replied. "We'll find our own way. Thanks anyhow."

The room had three beds, a small table and a couple of chairs. Father had found it more difficult than any of us to adjust to our new circumstances. As he had the day before, he threw himself on one of the beds, fully dressed, and immediately fell into an uneasy sleep.

The next morning, with the landlord off at work, we inspected the building. It had one advantage over the Hryniewicz house. With so many other families living here, no one paid much attention to us, so we had a certain degree of privacy.

"Let's think practically," I said. "The first problem is food. We need to buy the basic things, and then there's the cooking. I don't even know how to make a glass of tea."

"Well, you just buy the food," said father. "I know how to cook." This was a complete surprise. An orthodox Jew, the head of an orthodox household, he was used to being pampered by his wife and daughter.

"You know how to cook?" all three sons asked in unison.

"I'll prove it to you as soon as there's any food around here."

"Who'll do the shopping?" Abo asked.

"It'll be best if Wilo does it," I said, thinking aloud. "He looks like a shaygetz," a Gentile boy. "He's blond and blue-eyed, and he speaks Polish well."

"Also, he's got a good head on his shoulders," said Abo.

"It'll be fun," said Wilo, beaming. He must have thought that it was time to do his share for the family.

"You'll have to do a few things first," I said. "We don't have enough money, so you'll have to find a black-market buyer and sell him this old Russian gold coin. Of course, since you're young, he'll try to cheat you. You'll have to learn today's price of gold."

"I'm used to spotting black marketeers, I did it in the Judenlager." he boasted.

If you run into a Jew in disguise, be careful, there are informers everywhere." I advised. "All right, then. Once you have the Ukrainian money in your pocket, take a stroll through the market and see what food you can buy that we can use."

"I'll tell you what we need," said father. "You've got to buy bread, butter, milk, eggs and onions. Those will be the staples. Then, if you see dried peas and beans, kasha, carrots, beets and fruit, buy them, too."

Thus Wilo had his first solo adventure. He went to the market twice that morning. On the first trip, he sold a gold coin at a very good price, and brought home the first part of the shopping list. Then he returned for the remaining goods. The entire load would have been too much for him to carry in one trip. Our group of make-believe strangers was beginning to function properly.

Twenty-four hours later, in self-imposed confinement,

we were coming down with cabin fever. "This is exactly what happened to Misza," I said. "He's been living like this for close to a month, and by now he must be losing his mind. We can't let that happen to us."

"Do you want to know how I feel about it?" said Abo. "I think you should go to Misza and tell him about our situation. He might have some advice. He's been seeing people and talking to people."

"I wouldn't count on it," I replied. "But we've got nothing to lose by seeing him. I'll go this evening."

"Can I come with you?" Wilo implored. He was even more restless than the adults, and badly needed to move around. I thought about it for a while and said, "What the hell. I'll take you along."

The walk seemed much shorter than it had seemed two nights earlier, perhaps because the neighborhood was already somewhat familiar.

Misza had some news. "Imagine," he said, "I saw Juzek. He just arrived with his group from Lvov. He mentioned something about you—you're wanted by the Gestapo there. They've put notices up around the city. You're a dangerous fugitive."

I had an uneasy feeling in my stomach. I hadn't expected this sort of news.

"It must have been Ryzewskyj," I said angrily. "I'll pay that bastard back some day."

"Oh, something else! A guy from Lvov moved into our old room yesterday."

"My God, it might be my cousin Shmuel! I gave him the Hryniewiczs' address before we left."

"Can I do something?" pleaded Wilo. "I can run over

there and find out whether it's Shmuel. I know my way around by now."

It wasn't a bad idea. Off he went, and as we waited impatiently for him to return I explained my family's predicament to Misza.

"I don't think there's any way I can get back to Lvov for my mother. I get shivers just thinking about it. What can I tell my father?"

"You'll have to tell him how it is." Misza, as usual, was practical and pessimistic. "Unless you want to commit suicide by returning to Lvov."

Wilo was back within the hour. "It is Shmuel!" he announced. "I saw him through the window, and he talked to me in the orchard. He says that at first, he was afraid to travel; that's why he didn't come with us. Then he saw that things were getting worse in the Judenlager, and he changed his mind. He came here with Juzek's group and went to the Hryniewiczs' to see us. He says it's awful now in Lvov. The SS has put a double cordon around the Judenlager, just like they did at the Janowska camp. There are rumors they're going to liquidate everyone."

Neither father nor Abo would learn the bad news that night, because both were fast asleep when Wilo and I returned.

But the truth had to come out eventually. "We're all mature people," I began as we sat down to a splendid breakfast cooked by father. "Another trip back to Lvov is out of the question for me. I'm on the Gestapo's list and they are searching for me."

No one said anything. Continuous terror had desensitized us. No matter how heartbreaking the news might be, we were used to taking it with no show of emotion. Only father gasped in despair: "Oh, my poor wife!"

"We'll have to bite our lips and accept our fate," I said. "What must be will be, there's no way of knowing the future. It's the only life we've been granted. Let's try to live it."

"In other words, act as if everything is normal," Abo commented. "Wilo should keep buying food, father should cook it, and I should clean the room."

"More or less. Listen. To make our life closer to normal, let's try to find jobs—you and me, Stanislaw Nowak and Piotr Siminski."

"A real job?" Abo was clearly confounded. "Like the one I had at Ryzewskyj's?"

"Not like what we had at Ryzewskyj's, but honest-to-goodness employment. If we find work, we'll be completely different from most of the Jews hiding here. We'll go out as Poles or Volksdeutsche, and we'll apply for jobs with a German construction company. Why shouldn't we? We've got the papers. If they were good enough to get us here, then they must be good enough to land us jobs. With all the stamps and official signatures, I don't think anyone will question our credentials. Besides, we have the Organization Todt uniforms—and, anyway, we've got Jewish brains under our German army caps."

With that, I picked up the day's paper and turned to the "Help Wanted" page.

"I don't believe it! Look at all these ads! One construction company after another. All of them German."

"What are they looking for?" Abo asked.

"Never mind! We'll learn whatever we have to learn. Here, somebody's looking for an assistant engineer."

"So? What do you know about engineering?"

"Well, I had six months of drafting in the gymnasium."

"Five years ago."

"Have no fear! I'll learn on the job. The only thing that counts right now is getting hired."

"And where is that job?"

"Away from Dnepropetrovsk. In the southern Ukraine, in a town called Dolginzewo. Look at this huge ad!" I shoved the paper under his nose. "Leonhard Wening Bauunternehmung — Leonhard Wening Construction. It sounds fantastic. They need all kinds of people."

"What do you know about Dolginzewo? Where is it?"

"I don't know the first thing about it. But I'll learn everything I need to know. Obviously the company, or whatever it is, isn't in Dnepropetrovsk. That's one thing in its favor. As soon as I know where to go, you and I will take the train, or get there some other way, and apply at the personnel office."

"And what do you plan to do with Mr. Tyszkiewicz and little Stasio?"

"For the time being, they'll stay here. Wilo will buy supplies, and father will continue cooking. Four people living together is one thing; two is something else. With the two of us out, they'll be less conspicuous, don't you think?"

"So, once we're in Dolginzewo, all our chances will improve?"

"Well, they'll be better. Remember, we don't have that much gold. We need some income."

The discussion had unsettled father. "How will we be able to manage, with you and Abo gone?"

"We have to leave. The four of us can't stay together. It's too dangerous. Besides, you and Wilo will have to move eventually anyway. Think of us as going on a mission as meraglim, like the ancient biblical spies." I said, "We have to scout out the dangers. But as soon as we're settled, we'll get you to Dolginzewo. Meanwhile, you'll have to manage as best you can."

"And how about the valuables? Are you going to take them with you? You'll need money."

"I'm sure we'll need money, but we won't take the valuables with us. We'll take a few personal belongings, that's all. You'll keep the gold pieces we have left. You'll need them for food and rent, and Wilo is quite good at dealing with the money-changers at the market. Look! This is the way it's got to be."

It hurt, but there really was no other way. Father was a mature man; even though he couldn't accept the situation immediately, he would do so eventually. And Wilo was enthusiastic. "This means I might get a real job sooner or later," he mused.

After investigation, we established that Dolginzewo was a tiny town along the rail line, eight kilometers from a larger town called Krivoi Rog. The latter name was familiar to Poles because of the seventeenth-century Cossack rebellion against the king of Poland. Both towns were in a heavily industrialized area surrounded by iron mines, about one hundred and fifty kilometers south of Dnepropetrovsk.

We came to a decision quickly. Abo and I would apply for work at the Wening Company. Before that, I sent Wilo to Shmuel with the message that he could move in with father and stay while we were gone.

Shmuel declined the offer. "I feel safe when I'm alone," was his reply. Some time later, we learned that Shmuel had brought a money belt filled with gold coins with him from Lvov, and counted on money to save his life. Maybe he was right; we thought we were right. No one could tell at that point whose actions would turn out to be the right ones.

####### ||| ||| ||| ||| ||| |||

CHAPTER

8

Disguises

U KRAINIANS WHO WANTED to travel east or south didn't use public transportation. Perhaps it was to save money, or perhaps it wasn't feasible, with all the trains packed with soldiers and war materiel. Instead, travelers would gather at strategic spots along the highways outside the city. There they waited, sometimes for hours, for a lift on a military truck.

Abo and I hugged Wilo and father goodbye, and left the house. It was early in the morning, but most workers had already gone to their jobs and the streets were empty. We had decided to go without uniforms, so Abo was dressed in a light summer suit while I wore my brown leather jacket. With our meager belongings in our knapsacks we marched along the road following the signs to Krivoi Rog, carefully avoiding places where large groups of Ukrainians waited for lifts.

We were lucky. After only half an hour of thumbing for a ride, a military truck stopped for us. The driver, a Wehrmacht soldier, asked where we were headed.

"Krivoi Rog!" I shouted over the noise of the engine. "That's where our work site is."

"Hop on!" he said. "We'll get you there."

It was hard to believe that no one asked for identification, that no one wanted to know who we were working for or to see proof that we were indeed workers, and not Jews. We sat on a heap of tires, clinging to the sides of the truck as it lurched over the bumps and potholes.

Five hours later, we reached Krivoi Rog. Now we had to find our way to Dolginzewo. We saw a road sign indicating that it was only a few kilometers away, so we decided to walk.

"What are we going to say when we get there?" Abo asked.

"Not we," I replied. "Me, I'll go in to explore. I'll discuss jobs. Then, if I'm successful, I'll tell them about you."

"What will you say? They want skilled workers, not laborers."

"How do you know what they want? I'll play it by ear. But I think I'll try for something to do with engineering."

We ate our sandwiches and washed them down with water from a well by the side of the road and walked on to enter Dolginzewo. It was clear that this was a railroad town. We'd soon learn that only a couple of kilometers down the track was a major depot, Kaganowicze, with a huge repair shop and a complete switching yard.

"Even if we do find work," Abo continued as we walked on, "who knows how hard it'll be to find a room?" The town consisted of a row of three-story housing projects and a number of private homes.

"Let's worry about jobs first," I said, and noticed something else about the town. "This place must not have a sewer system. Look at all those outhouses! It's like the countryside near Lvov."

Farther on we noticed a large sign indicating the Leonhard Wening offices. The main door was wide open.

"Hold my knapsack Abo. Keep a good distance, and say a prayer." I smoothed my crew cut, buttoned my jacket and went in.

I sought out the manager's office and knocked. A voice answered, "Come in!"

A short man, hunchbacked and bespectacled sat behind the desk. He stared inquisitively at me.

"Good afternoon, sir. My name is Nowak. I'm a Volksdeutscher of Polish origin. Basically, I'm from Lvov, but lately I've been living in Dnepropetrovsk. I saw your ad there," I said, and waved the page from the newspaper. "I'd like to apply for a position."

"How nice," said the hunchback in a soft, pleasant voice. "Please, take a seat."

I sat down and, without being asked, I handed over my documents.

The man perused them before introducing himself.

"My name is Kreutzer. I'm the head of personnel. Our boss, of course, is Mr. Wening, but he's on vacation in his hometown, Zürndorf, near Nürnberg. Mr. Karl Thiel, a gentleman from the Sudetenland, is the general manager in his absence. So, now that you know everything about us, maybe you can tell me a few things about yourself."

"I was an engineering student at the polytechnic school in Lvov," I lied. "I would have finished if it hadn't been for the war. But I'm a good learner. If you give me a chance, I could become a very good engineering assistant."

"So that's what you want. I appreciate your honesty." Kreutzer was so polite that it was difficult for me to identify him with the Germans. "Incidentally, you speak German well. Do you know any other languages? Ukrainian? Russian?"

"Both. And Polish."

"And you're Volksdeutsch? Everybody nowadays seems to be Volksdeutsch. Maybe you and I are relatives." That was said in jest, I was sure. "Well, anyway, we need a good man. There might be a spot for you — a construction supervisor. You'll have to translate instructions from German to Russian, or Ukrainian, or whatever it is the local workers speak. Then you'll have to make sure they do what they are told to do. And because you want to be an engineering assistant, I'll assign you to help our road engineer, Adam. He's a Pole, too. Let's find out if two Poles will work it out between themselves. You'll be paid well. As to the living arrangements, you'll do what our other employees do — eat in the mess hall and sleep in one of our dormitories — no charge to you. Is that satisfactory?"

"Very! I'd like to ask a small favor."

"Yes?"

"There's another Polish fellow who came here with me, Piotr Siminski. I've known him a while. He's young and not very experienced, but he's a good worker and willing to learn. And he speaks German, Polish, and Ukrainian, too."

"Where is he?"

"He's waiting outside."

"Well, then, let me talk to him."

I stepped outside and waved to Abo. Even though we had gone over our new story carefully I could tell that he was still afraid.

He needn't have been, however, as Kreutzer was easy to deal with. He asked Abo a few questions, glanced at his papers and told him that he was hired. He also told him that he would eat in the mess hall and sleep in the dormitory.

After that, Kreutzer showed us around. He introduced us to several German employees, some of them former soldiers who had been wounded and now worked at light jobs. I forgot every name as soon as it was spoken, but somehow I retained the impression that they were all called Hans or Otto.

Abo and I ate at the same table that evening, but made sure to sit away from one another. In the dormitory, my bunk was far from his. Those were preventive measures. We had to be sure that no one would recognize us as brothers.

I believe that was the best day we had ever spent

under Nazi rule. Nevertheless, I had trouble sleeping. Adam, the Polish engineer I would assist, lived in a private house. I hadn't met him yet. I was afraid of Poles. Like Ukrainians, they were much better than Germans at uncovering Jews who pretended to be Aryan.

In the morning, one of the many Ottos woke everyone up. He must have had a bad dream or stepped out of his bunk left foot first, as the saying went, because he was in an awful mood. He went down the aisle, proceeding toward the latrine, cursing wildly and kicking one bunk after another.

"He must be a Bavarian peasant," I said to Abo as we ran into each other on the way to the bathroom. "I can tell by his accent and vocabulary."

After a shower and a shave, we dressed, and downstairs in the mess hall, we met Herr Thiel, the boss in Wening's absence.

"I hear from Mr. Kreutzer that he's hired a new supervisor. You two are the only new faces around. Which one is Mr. Nowak?"

I stepped forward. "Well, I suppose you'll have to do," Thiel said after looking me over. Poking his finger at Abo, he added, "And this fellow will go to the construction site in Kaganowicze."

With that, Abo was dismissed, while I followed the heavy set German to meet Adam.

Adam, my immediate supervisor turned out to be a handsome man in his late thirties, of medium height, with dark hair and warm brown eyes. He was serious and reserved as he shook my hand and said, "Welcome to Dolginzewo." Even when we were alone, he would shy away from personal topics. He neither mentioned his family nor asked about mine. There was no talk about friends, hometowns or even the engineering schools we had attended. All this made me feel much more at ease.

"Colleague," Adam began. It was a title used by Polish professionals whenever they addressed each other. "Let me introduce you to your new duties. We'll get out the land measuring instruments and start our normal workday."

We went into a shack where Adam gave me the instruments, one by one. Each time he handed me a piece of equipment, he pronounced its name slowly and clearly, as though he was teaching a foreigner a new language. And the terms did sound foreign. "Stadia Rod. Subtense Bar. Range Finder. And here, colleague, is our most basic tool, the common surveying instrument with telescopic sight — our Transit."

Carrying the tools of my new trade, I followed the engineer. When we reached an area where some hundred Ukrainian laborers toiled with picks, spades and shovels, Adam stopped.

"All right, then! We'll begin by measuring the grade of the areas around the railroad depot," he announced.

I had no idea how to begin, and decided to substitute eagerness for expertise.

"I was an engineering student, when . . ."

"You don't have to explain," Adam said curtly. "You'll learn as we go along. I'm sure I'll be a good teacher. I've got a lot of patience." He looked pensively at me. "If there's anything I have left, it's patience."

Here was a strange person, I thought. He does not act

the way I expect he would. He was an experienced engineer — we had soon taken care of numerous chores, and Adam's deep knowledge of his profession had become obvious — and yet he was so gentle. He simply did not act Polish. Suddenly it became clear to me. Adam was a *Jew* in disguise.

I am afraid I was staring and that unsettled him. For a moment he cast his eyes down and appeared unsure. Pole or Jew, he seemed to have the same reservation about me that I'd had about him.

I made an effort to break the spell. "What kind of work are they doing in the depot?"

"Depot? Oh, yes." Adam regained his composure. "That's where the cars are repaired. It's what Dolginzewo is known for."

In that one day, I learned more than I had in months at the gymnasium. Adam was indeed, a willing teacher and I was an avid student.

"Well," he said after many hours of work, "let's call it a day. Please be kind enough to take the instruments back to the shack while I go see Mr. Thiel. This is the routine," he explained. "At the end of the day, I have to make a report." A report seemed ominous. I wondered what he would say about me. My fears proved unfounded. Thiel approached me later that evening, saying, "Congratulations, Mr. Nowak! Adam had some very good things to say about you."

Abo, too, had a very good day. He told me that he had served as a translator for the Ukrainian laborers and their German foremen, and had begun to learn something about road building.

I suggested a walk after dinner. He agreed. Dolginzewo was a new world as far as we were concerned. As we strolled through the unpaved streets, it seemed rustic and peaceful. The air was filled with the aroma of fruit trees in bloom, and we could hear children playing. I thought of Dnepropetrovsk with its hidden dangers, then my thoughts went to the Judenlager.

"I have a feeling of nightmarish unreality," Abo said to me. "We live in the midst of horror, and yet somewhere, there's a real world inhabited by real people. They're sad or joyful, happy or unhappy, they're normal. And I can't tell whether Dolginzewo is real and Lvov a nightmare, or what is real.

"Mr. Piotr Siminski is either a poet or a philosopher," I replied, laughing.

It was good to be able to laugh; we seldom did.

"It's hard to imagine," Abo said. "We've acted a lot of parts, put on a lot of disguises, but this is the first time we've been able to express simple happiness."

"Maybe this isn't a disguise. Maybe this is the real us. Maybe, after all, I am Nowak, and you are Siminski, and not two Jewish brothers."

"Shhh!" Abo hushed me. Suddenly there were no more colors, sounds or aromas. Grayness — our real world — enveloped us again.

"Let me tell you about Adam," I said. "One of these days, I'll introduce you to him. But you'll have to be on your toes. It might be my imagination, but I think he's one of us. There's a certain tension between us. I can't feel at ease with him, and I think he's scared of me. But he's a good man."

After working with Adam for a week, I learned enough

to perform some tasks independently. Accordingly, Thiel transferred me to a different construction site and promoted me to surveyor. Although still insecure with the instruments, I managed to do satisfactory work.

Now every evening, Adam and I would report to Thiel's office together and the three of us would make plans for the following day. Abo confessed to me that he often thought of us. In his imagination, he saw three heads bent over a chart. "They're all wearing masks — Nowak, Adam, maybe even Mr. Thiel?" He was right. I remembered a movie theater in Lvov, the Palace, a gorgeous work of architecture. Above the huge velvet curtain, two plaster masks were affixed to the wall, the ancient Greek masks of tragedy and comedy. Each of us wore a mask now, I thought.

Abo worked his way up quickly and soon, he was a functionary, one of the many construction foremen. Life seemed to have smiled on the two of us.

The top man, Wening, returned from vacation, and that evening called a meeting of all supervisors. He was a tall, hefty man with eyeglasses and rough-hewn features. At first he sat, then stood up behind his desk. His voice was hoarse and his accent Bavarian.

"Meine Herren!" he addressed the assembly. "Gentlemen! I have good news to share with you. The Ministry of Railroads has awarded me a contract for the construction of tracks and of barracks for railway employees. So, as of now, while the company will keep an office in Zürndorf, our headquarters will be moved to Dolginzewo.

It was good news indeed. Wening, an old Nazi party member, had some excellent connections in the government. A contract of this size must have been lucrative and would provide employment for many people. The management, generally older German civilians or disabled veterans, would grow in number. More supervisors would be hired. Even more Ukrainian laborers would be employed near their home, instead of being deported as slaves for munitions factories deep in Germany. Besides, although Wening's attitude was generally patronizing, and on occasion he would not hesitate to slap a Ukrainian in the face, there was much less physical abuse in this company than in other German businesses in the southern Ukraine. To show how egalitarian he was, Wening got himself a girlfriend — a young Ukrainian mother of three — who, in exchange for sexual favors, was put in charge of the kitchen.

One morning, he called me into his office. "Take a seat, Herr Nowak," he urged with all the politeness he could muster. I sat down.

"Yes sir, Herr Wening!"

"I've got some interesting news for you," he said. I felt shivers down my spine. An hour before, I had seen a Gestapo car leave the premises.

"Yes sir!" I repeated.

"Your co-worker Adam has left us. He received an offer for an engineering position in the general government territory, somewhere near Warsaw, that was too good to be refused."

"Oh?" This was an unpleasant surprise. Though I was never fully at ease with Adam, I liked working with him and I could always count on his advice. And to leave without saying goodbye? I assumed that my first impression had been correct, that he was a Jew. He must have guessed the same about my brother and me, decided that Dolginzewo had become too dangerous, and managed to disappear.

"Well, then, Mr. Nowak! That leaves only you. There is no third possibility. I hereby appoint you as Adam's replacement."

It was a bolt from a clear sky. I felt joy yet panic. I knew Napoleon's saying that every soldier carries a marshal's baton in his knapsack, but I would never have imagined *this*. A Jew masquerading as a Pole, pretending to be a Volksdeutsch, without the required four years at the polytechnic, and barely any experience, was suddenly the engineer in charge of a large Nazi construction company most of whose business was done a few hundred kilometers behind the front line. I was relieved that the visit by the Gestapo had nothing to do with me, I looked forward to a higher salary, but I was terrified by my new responsibilities.

"But, Herr Wening . . ." I began to protest.

"No, no! Don't thank me! Adam has described you as a person of exceptional ability and a hard worker. And our Mr. Kreutzer told me that his parents and your grandparents both came from Silesia, and that he considers you as some sort of third cousin. So you will be my construction consultant and work inspector. Your new position means that you will have the company car at your disposal, as well as a chauffer."

There was no way to change his mind, and I decided to make the most of the opportunity.

"Herr Wening, sir! Now that you have mentioned the

car and the chauffer, I'd like to ask you for a really big favor."

"Go ahead! Ask!" He was in a good mood.

"May I have a room in a private house, please? The bunk in the dormitory is bad for my back."

"I don't see why not. But we can arrange it only when I hear that an officially requisitioned place is available. When that happens, I'll issue an order to place you there. Incidentally, our foremen have already been advised of your new position. My suggestion is that you have a hearty breakfast, and then order the chauffer to take you around all the construction sites. That way, you'll meet the foremen, get an idea of the work we're doing. This will be your first inspection tour."

In the mess hall, I tried to digest my scrambled eggs and sausage along with my new situation all at the same time. It was a difficult mixture to metabolize. "A nice fix," I said to myself. I'm not an engineer! I wanted to remain inconspicuous!" My mother would have capped the situation with an "Oy vay is mir!"

That day I had a round of meetings with the foremen and listened to complaints and suggestions from Ukrainian workers.

"I'm glad Adam's gone," one of the foremen declared. "He gave me the creeps." "Ah, now," I said. "That's exactly what you'll say about me when I'm gone. "Never!" the foreman swore. "You're one of us boys."

Later, a group of Ukrainians approached their new chief. "We're happy for you, Pan Nowak. How are things in Lvov? Are any Jews left?" their spokesman inquired in a candid expression of hatred for the Jews by men who, until a short time before had been members of the Soviet Communist society, in which, they said, all people are brothers. I grinned in response; I wanted to play my part properly.

"No, Stefan. No more Jews in Lvov. The Germans did a good job. And nice Ukrainian boys like you helped them."

I went for another stroll with my brother that evening. I gave him an account of my first day as chief engineer for the L. Wening Company, including the questions about the Jews of Lvov.

Abo said it made him sick to his stomach to hear Ukrainians talk about how they hated Jews. Of course, his stomach might also have been reacting to the several pounds of grapes we had swallowed during our walk! Then I told him about my request for private quarters. He saw the wisdom in it, but I could tell that he also thought it was a bit unfair. I was going my separate way, and from now on he would have to count more and more on his own resourcefulness.

"It might help us a little," he said, trying to put the best face on the change. "The less we're seen together, the less people will notice our resemblance."

The next day, I made it official. I let it be known to anybody who was interested that I wanted a room. My particular targets were the Ukrainian employees who had homes in Dolginzewo.

Sure enough, a couple of days later a woman approached me in the yard in front of the office.

"I hear you wish a place to stay," she said. "There's a furnished room in my house that I'd like to rent to a nice tenant." She gauged me with her blue eyes and instinctively touched her smooth, dark-blond hair with both hands, as though to make sure it was all there. "It's already on the German requisition list. I live there with my aunt and my four-year-old son. I believe I am a widow," she added. "The last time I saw my husband was two years ago, when the Red Army retreated. He was a soldier. I haven't heard from his since."

She was pretty, and seemed not much older than I. "Who told you I needed a room?" I asked; best to be careful. "Why, I work right here," she said. "In the warehouse. Everbody knows you're looking for a place to live."

After dinner, I went to see Lida's place. The house was simple, the room large and clean although scantily furnished. Generally speaking it should have been all right, except . . .

"Except that you have no running water, and, what's worse, no toilet. Not even an outhouse! How can you people live like this?"

She was genuinely surprised.

"Nobody has running water or a toilet, except maybe the people who live in those big modern buildings." There were several of those in Dolginzewo. "But what do you need all that for? There's a well outside, and you have a basin in your room where you can wash. As for the toilet, people have been using the cornfields in back of the house for generations. It's convenient for you, and it's good for the corn."

I took the room, but had my reservations about the facilities.

Several evenings later, Abo helped me move my few

belongings to Lida's place. We used the company car, of course, because she lived a good distance from the office.

"Guest in the house, God in the house!" Lida met us at the threshold with the old Slavic greeting.

Instead of the traditional bread and salt with which ancient Slavs would receive a caller, we had a glass of tea with Lida and her aunt.

"My husband, blessed be his soul, was sent to Siberia in 1930," the old woman said, sipping her tea and sighing. "Times were bad then, and they're worse now. Look at what's happened to our people! Some of our boys went off to fight with the Red Army, and the others were taken to Germany. The Germans killed some of them, along with the Jews who didn't run away with the Red Army. I don't even feel sorry for the damned Jews! They had a good life here before."

"They must have been Communists," I said, trying to sound scornful. "Who knows? They might even have been NKVD people."

"No, not our Jews," Lida said. "They were simple people. Watch repairers, cobblers, state-store managers."

"Were any of them friends of yours?" Abo asked.

"No. They stuck together, they only associated with each other. That's why we didn't like them."

Abo pressed on. "Disliked? Not hated?"

"There may have been some hatred. I don't know."

I broke the silence that followed. "I've been thinking. I'm going to build us a decent outhouse in the back yard. And this young man, Piotr, will help me, whether he likes it or not."

And so it was that during the next few weeks, my brother and I used all our free time, and every board we could make disappear from the Wening lumberyard, to build an outhouse in Lida's back yard.

Time passed quickly. By September 1943 I was an expert in my new occupation, and Abo in his. I so identified with my new style of life that my German accent and vocabulary were becoming more Bavarian and, like the rest of the German supervisors, I had acquired a Ukrainian girlfriend.

"It's not what you're thinking," I assured Abo time and time again. "Lida is not my mistress. I just want everybody to think she is. Then no one will imagine I'm a Jew."

"But you live under the same roof; you take her to the movies; you walk holding hands; you bring gifts for her son. What else do you do?"

"To tell the truth, I do feel the need, and she's willing. But how can I? She'd recognize me as Jew."

"You're right. But why does she accept the situation?"

"She does because I told her I have a fiancée in Lvov and that I'm a one-woman man."

All the time we had been in Dolginzewo, we had not heard from father and Wilo. It had been less than three months, but it seemed like a lifetime. We worried a lot, but didn't dare mail a letter.

I sometimes wondered if they were still alive. Because of our fears neither Abo nor I could bear to raise the subject. We never mentioned them, but both of us were nearly consumed by anxiety.

I had become close to the office staff, which, besides

Wening's personal secretary and Kreutzer, consisted of several young people from the southern Ukraine. Some of the Ukrainians, it developed, hated the Germans virulently. One of them, a pleasant man named Vassily, was the firm's courier.

"Vassily's being sent on an errand to Dnepropetrovsk," Abo said casually to me one day.

"Are you absolutely sure?" I asked. "For how long?"

"He told me so himself. For a few days."

"I trust him," I said. "I'll ask him to deliver some money to father, and a note."

Abo was stunned. He hadn't thought that I would take such a risk. It would put all our lives in jeopardy. Nonetheless, he seemed pleased by my determination to get news to father and Wilo.

I have a favor to ask you. "There's an old fellow," I said to Vassily, "a friend's father, an old Pole from Lvov, who lives in Dnepropetrovsk. I'd like to send him a note and little money."

"Say no more! I like the way you Poles stick together. I'll be happy to do it."

Of course, doing a favor for his superior would be in Vassily's best interest, but beyond that, he was a nice, accommodating sort.

Less than a week later, he was back from Dnepropetrovsk. Not only had he delivered the money and the letter, but he had brought a note in reply.

"I saw the old man," he said. "I also met a little boy, Stasio, who stays with him. They both thank you for the money. They asked me to tell you that they're fine. The boy wanted your address, so I gave it to him. I hope you don't mind."

I didn't mind at all. Had Abo and I been drinkers, we would have celebrated that evening with a bottle of vodka.

╫ ╫ ╫ ╫ ╫ ╫

CHAPTER

9

___

Reunion

ANOTHER WEEK had passed. "I'm tired, I think I'll call it a day," I said, stretching lazily. Abo and I had just finished one of the rare dinners at which we risked sitting next to each other in the mess hall. I rose and left.

Abo lingered. It was only six o'clock, much too early to head for the dormitory. A young boy appeared in the doorway. He was small, slender and pale. At first, Abo didn't make the connection. Then, suddenly, he recognized him.

"Stasio!" he cried anxiously. "Stasio!" Heedless of the other diners, Wilo moved toward Abo, but he stopped, looked around cautiously and then put on as much nonchalance as he could muster.

They wanted to fall into each other's arms, but shook hands quietly. "I'm hungry," was Wilo's simple but natural opening. Abo took him to the kitchen, where one of the female cooks gave him a large plate of food. "Eat, malchik," little one, she said. "You look so undernourished!" When Wilo had eaten as much as he could, they left the mess hall.

"Let's go see Nowak!" Abo said. He was happy and excited, but he didn't want to hear Wilo's story until I could be there to hear it too. Lida led them to our room. I was flustered for a moment when I saw who was there, and, expecting the worst, but restraining myself asked, "How are things?"

"Everything's all right," Wilo replied laconically. "Then welcome, Stasio!" I said. "Have you had dinner?"

"A few minutes ago, in the mess hall."

"That's good. So, why don't we all go out for a walk?"

I stopped at the door of Lida's rooms. "Oh, Lida! I'd like you to meet someone. This is Stasio, the son of my parents' friends. We're going for a walk, and then I'd like him to spend a few nights with me. He'll be leaving in a day or two."

We walked down Dolginzewo's main street, and Wilo gave us the latest news. Despite what he'd said earlier, things were not so good.

"We can't live in Dnepropetrovsk any longer," he told us. "Do you remember just before we left Lvov? Well, the same thing is happening. Germans, Ukrainians, even Poles are combing the city for Jews. They're shooting them on the spot, hanging them, torturing and deporting people. Misza was heading from one hideout to another when the

Gestapo caught him. Shmuel's safe so far, but now he's got a bad kidney infection. He's in pain, and he can't move freely. And he's afraid to see a doctor — after all, he's circumcized."

"I see. I see," I repeated while I tried to think. "The four of us together in Dolginzewo might be bad news, but it looks as if it's the only way. Tomorrow morning, I'll give you food and money, and you'll return to Dnepropetrovsk. Tell father he shouldn't worry. Coming to Dolginzewo will not endanger us. We'll handle it. As soon as the two of you arrive, I'll get you a room in another part of town so no one can suspect we're family."

We started counting the days after Wilo left. Time simply wasn't moving. During the day, work pushed our anxiety to the back of our minds. But at night we couldn't sleep, now looking forward to father's arrival, now trembling at the thought of it.

Two weeks passed without a word.

"Something awful must have happened," said Abo. I agreed. "He must have been caught by the Ukrainians on his way back to Dnepropetrovsk."

At long last, late one night, the two of them appeared in the dormitory. They looked awful, bruised, filthy, terrified, and so thin.

"Careful, don't wake anybody," Abo said softly. "Let's get out of here and go to Nowak's."

I was shocked by the sight. "My God!" I exclaimed. "What has happened to you?"

Father, his cap pushed back, his jacket collar up, a cigarette butt hanging from his mouth, grinned and replied, "So, Mr. Nowak! So how are things?"

"Make yourselves at home. I'll have to talk with Lida."

Of course, Lida and her aunt had seen our strange callers.

"The starik," Lida said, "looks very bad. So small and skinny, he hardly looks alive. And the malchik looked much healthier two weeks ago. Have they been in an accident?"

"In a way. Look, Lida, considering the condition they're in and the hour, I'd like them to spend the night with me. The old man is my best friend's father. The kid can sleep on the floor; he's used to it."

"Well," she said somewhat reluctantly, "it is your room, after all."

The new arrivals washed outside at the well, telling their story as they did so.

"I urged father to leave Dnepropetrovsk as soon as I got back, but he wouldn't listen to me," Wilo complained. "He said he didn't want to put you in danger."

"Big deal!" father whispered as he dried himself. "We left yesterday morning."

"Yes, but by then all hell had broken loose. At ten in the morning, that guy Rubin, your friend from Lvov, came to warn us that he'd just seen a Gestapo truck nearby, full of Jews. As he was telling us about it, we heard the truck go by. He ran off. We grabbed our packs and jumped out the back window. We ran through fields — I don't know for how long — until we got to the highway."

"There was a crowd of hitchhikers there," father interrupted, "so I assumed this was the place to get a lift. Wilo confirmed it. I didn't want to talk to Ukrainians, so I suggested that we post ourselves a little further up. I also thought a truck would rather pick up two people by themselves than a whole crowd."

"We waited for two hours," said Wilo. "The trucks never stopped near us — always down the road, where the crowd was."

"I was wrong," father admitted. "When one crowd was gone, a new one started forming. Then, all of a sudden, there was that hoodlum, our landlord's cousin. He took one look at us — he must have connected us with the Gestapo dragnet — and yelled, 'stop those Jews!' I don't know why, but he was the only one who ran after us."

"We ran like rabbits." Wilo savored the scene.

"Finally," father said, beaming, "I had an idea. We dropped our bundles, and he stopped to pick them up. He must have been expecting Jews to have gold! We got back to the highway, and this time we got a ride almost immediately. They said they were headed for Krivoi Rog. We had to get off the truck about fifty kilometers along the road, though — because they needed to go in another direction. It was late by that time, so we spent the night in a cornfield."

Wilo continued the story. "In the morning," he said, "we started walking south. After hours of walking, we arrived at a village. A peasant woman fed us and gave us milk to drink. Ukrainians can be very generous — sometimes."

"We rested a little," continued father, "and then walked some more. In the afternoon, a tractor gave us a ride almost as far as Dolginzewo. We had to walk the last few kilometers, but here we are!"

"Thank God for it," I added. "Now, let's get some sleep. In the morning, I'll take Wilo with me, maybe I'll find him a job. And you, Mr. Tyszkiewicz, will take it easy until we find lodging for you somewhere safe."

"Easy? How can I take it easy? With all that walking and running, my old hernia has returned — on both sides. And I've got bleeding hemorrhoids as well."

"Bad, but that's the least of our problems right now. More important is to figure out what we can do tomorrow."

Abo went back to the dormitory. We met again in the morning, at breakfast in the mess hall. I had Wilo with me.

"I'll talk to our Mr. Kreutzer," I said. "He's convince-able. He might assign him to a journeyman as an apprentice. Maybe that fellow Duchenko, the master carpenter. He's a good man."

Wilo didn't even hear me talking. He was busy devouring a huge portion of eggs with sausage and a thick slice of bread, and washing it all down with tea. When he finished, he went to the kitchen for more, and the woman who had fed him two weeks before piled more eggs on his plate.

After breakfast, I went to see Kreutzer while Wilo waited outside. Soon I was able to motion to him to come into the office. "This is Stasio Grabowski," I told the personnel manager. "I knew his parents; they both died when a bomb hit their house. He's a bright boy, and I'm sure he'd make a good apprentice."

"I can tell you have something specific in mind." By now, Kreutzer was familiar with my tactics. "Who do you think he should work with?"

"Duchenko, the carpenter. The kid can learn a good trade."

Kreutzer sighed. "All right, all right! We can always use one more pair of hands." He turned to his secretary. "Please issue working papers for this young man. And put him on the payroll — minimum wage."

Next I introduced my brother to his new boss. "Stasio's an orphan," I said. "His parents used to be friends of my folks." Lies came out of my mouth like pristine truths.

Duchenko nodded. "I understand. I started out as an apprentice myself. It took me years to learn, but look at me now!" He pounded his chest with a heavy fist. "I'm a master craftsman!" He patted Wilo on the head. "Not to worry, malchik. I'll take care of you. You'll be like a son to me."

That was an achievement. Three brothers, three refugees from the Judenlager, eating at the same table in a German contractor's mess hall.

When I came home that evening, I found father sitting on a bench under an apple tree, basking in the setting sun. He inhaled the balmy September air with pleasure.

"It would have been perfect," he said as we entered the room, "if it weren't for that little monster."

"Are you talking about Lida's son?"

"Yes."

"What did he do to you?"

"All afternoon he kept throwing rotten apples at me. In the end, he climbed up the tree, sat on a branch over my head, and pissed all over me. I could have killed him, but I was afraid to do anything."

"What a nasty kid! But don't give it another thought. I'll get a room for you and Wilo elsewhere tomorrow."

Just then, there was a knock on the door. It was Lida. "I have to discuss something urgent with you." She looked worried.

"Come in, Lida."

"No. Not in your room." She pulled me by the arm and closed the door when we were outside.

"That old man," she whispered, "there's something wrong with him. You've got to get rid of him."

"What's the matter?" I blushed. Had she discovered that Mr. Tyszkiewicz was a Jew?

"This morning, I found the bedsheet soaked with blood. He must be very sick, and I'm afraid you might catch something from him. He's got to go!"

"Oh, that!" I laughed with relief. "That's nothing. He has bleeding hemorrhoids, that's all. Anyway, he'll move out tomorrow to a place of his own. Together with the kid."

"All right. But no later than tomorrow!"

I took the next day off. I had to find a room for my father and brother, and I had to do it in a few hours.

I started by talking to the local Ukrainians in the office. Then I went to talk to the kitchen staff. Everyone wanted to help, but the housing shortage was severe. Going from one person to another, I finally heard of something promising.

"I know two widowed sisters," a woman in the kitchen said. "They've been looking around for a decent tenant. Maybe you could try them."

It was already the middle of the afternoon when I

arrived at the address she gave me. It was a house off the main road, halfway between the company's offices and Lida's house — the best possible location. The room itself was large. The furnishings were modest, even by Dolginzewo standards — two beds, two chairs and a small cabinet. But it had two doors, one leading to the back yard — a real bonanza in case there was a sudden need to escape.

"I'll take it," I told the sisters. "I'll be back in a few hours. You'll have two tenants, an old man and a boy. They're nice, neat people."

Before bringing father and Wilo to the new place, I went to the outdoor market to buy such necessities as soap, toothbrushes, tooth powder, razors and kitchen utensils. Whatever father and Wilo had had were now the property of their Ukrainian pursuer in Dnepropetrovsk.

In the evening, the four of us walked to the widows' house. "This is a palace!" father exclaimed when we reached the one-family cottage. He really meant it. After the hell of the Judenlager and the purgatory of Dnepropetrovsk, this cottage was a paradise. "I wish your mother were here with me," he added, starting to cry. "My poor wife! God keep her in His mercy."

"I hope she's hiding with Rozia at the Prachtels' house," I said soothingly. "Such wonderful people! If all the Poles were like them, there'd be no ghetto and no deportations."

Abo interrupted. "I want to say something," he announced, addressing me. "It has to do with our situation here. On several occasions, people have noticed the resemblance between you and me. God forbid anyone should connect the four of us!"

"I understand," father said. "That's why I didn't want to come in the first place."

"But now you're here. We'll get by. Wilo has a job; Abo and I will help. There's only one thing we have to be careful about; we can meet only once in a while, and then we'll have to be absolutely sure that nobody follows or watches us."

From that point on, we were set in our daily routine. During breakfast in the mess hall, I could see Abo at one end of the table and Wilo at the other. After the meal, Abo would go to work as a foreman, Wilo to his job as Duchenko's apprentice, and I to Thiel's office to receive my assignment for the day. Then, with engineering equipment under both arms, I would get into the company car and head for my first construction site.

During the months that followed a subtle comradery developed between Ivan, the chauffeur, and me. Both of us would sometimes admit our dislike of the Nazis; in addition, I sensed that there might be a connection between Ivan and the seldom visible Russian partisans.

"Of course, I don't know when the war will end," Ivan once remarked. "But I can tell you this much: the Germans will be moving out of here soon."

"How soon?"

"The way I see it, it's a matter of months. It's September now, I'd guess by Christmas, or the beginning of 1944 at the latest."

"I wish you were a prophet."

"You can help me become one."

"Me? How?"

Ivan lowered his voice.

"By a little invisible sabotage. Screw them up where you can."

"I understand," I replied. "I'll see what I can do."

By now, my work had grown in importance. I measured land elevations in the area around Kaganowicze, and supervised repairs and installations of rails. I had the last word when there was a question of whether to use a bulldozer on a stretch of land, or to grade and level it with a crew of laborers, armed with spades and shovels.

Ivan continued one day, whispering. "You can see for yourself what's going on. Look at all the prefabricated workers' housing they're putting up in Dolginzewo. Some of the parts — the wooden walls, for example — they have brought in from the territory that's been evacuated. These barracks are meant for German railroad workers, the civilians who'll be retreating with the Wehrmacht and the Waffen SS. The army will be digging in here soon. Dolginzewo will be on the front line."

Occasionally, Thiel or even Wening himself would join me on inspection trips. Work was proceeding at top speed, and the owner wanted to see for himself the fruits of his government contracts.

A usual stop on these tours was Duchenko's shop. We would walk in as they were bent over the timber and planks, and Wilo would snap to attention before us. At another stop, we might run into Abo and his crew of ditch-diggers. Abo, clicking his heels, would rant like a robot: "Herr Thiel! Herr Nowak! Ich melde mich gehorsam!"

It was a strange masquerade, two men forced to give a military salute to their brother, address him as "Sir!" and call him by a name that wasn't his. It made us think about the contrast with the ghetto, the tragedy of being a Jew in these times, man's resilience under adversity, and something Darwin referred to as the survival of the fittest. Fitness, we discovered, meant craftiness as well as physical strength.

For example, I could show no favors to my brothers, lest our relationship be discovered. Once, when Abo was traveling with a German work crew on a train from Dolginzewo to Kaganowicze, he joined in a game of blackjack and was caught cheating at the cards by a German named Hans. Since I was also on the train, Hans appealed to me as the supervisor. I slapped Abo's face, hard. Fortunately, that satisfied Hans. A few days later, when we met father and told him the story, his comment was, "That slap saved Abo's life!"

The company had an official Dolmetscher, or interpreter, a local Volksdeutsche woman named Rose, but I did most of the interpreting on field visits with either of my two superiors. Thiel didn't like Rose. "She's promiscuous," he'd say, "and a drunk." As a German from Sudetenland, which until 1938 had belonged to Czechoslovakia, he was a sophisticated man who looked down on Rose and her German boyfriends. He referred to them sarcastically as Herrenvolk, "the master race," and in education and manners found them the equals of the local peasants. He found most of the firm's supervisors to be Bayerische Dummköpfe, "morons from Bavaria," and despised them even more, because of the foul language and brute force they used with the Ukrainians. "The people from Dolginzewo," he'd say time after time, "are stupid and filthy. They are pigs; they are sub-human. But nevertheless, one should never curse them or, even worse, beat them. It is ungentlemanly." In all this, Thiel never mentioned the plight of the Jews.

Wening, however, did not concern himself with his staff's manners. When he joined me on inspections, he was interested only in the progress we'd made on the contract.

"The work is going slowly," I would explain, "because the area I've got to grade has boulders and tree stumps. The earth itself is rock-hard, and the crews have to work under the most primitive conditions and only with hand tools."

A retired SS officer and active Nazi, Wening was a man of action. He wanted the work done, no matter what. If a laborer happened to be sick in bed, he'd curse the absent man and call him "ein verfluchter partisaner" — "a damned partisan." After that, he would order the local police to verify if the man was really sick and, if he was faking, to give him twenty lashes. Absentees would often be arrested, flogged and, at Wening's order, deported to Germany as slave laborers.

The owner had one quality that both Abo and I greatly appreciated, ignorance. This had made it possible for me to become chief engineer and for me to help Abo protect his workers by reporting as sick those whose illness would otherwise have to be vouched for by a physician.

There was just one Ukrainian laborer whom Abo did not want to protect, a man named Ivan Sapozhnik. Ivan was boorish and blunt, a giant of a man whose main occupation was repairing shoes but who had been drafted by Wening for construction work. In his instincts and actions, he was as primitive as Vlasov's Cossacks.

Whenever he got a willing audience, he would regale it with stories of how he had murdered Jews fleeing from the Germans. This was during the German army's Blitzkrieg into Russia, when it overran the Ukraine and Jews from the southern Ukrainian cities tried to flee deep into the Soviet Union.

"It was in a village at the other side of Krivoi Rog." He would wave in that town's direction. "There was a papa Jew, a mama Jew, and four little Jewish bastards. One by one, I grabbed them around the middle and lifted them like this" — he raised his powerful arms in the air — "and threw them down a mine shaft. At the bottom, there was a well filled with ice-cold water. And do you know what? They didn't even try to defend themselves! They just cried 'Oy, vay!' and said some prayers in Jewish. All I could catch was something like Shema Yisroel."

Abo discussed Ivan with me more than once. He felt that something should be done about him, and I agreed, saying, "He should pay for what he's done. He's a murderer, and he boasts about it. And the rest of them sit there and applaud." Finally, Abo decided to act, using Wening as his tool.

Ivan frequently missed work. Abo had never reported him, although he knew that when he missed work, it was to attend to his cobbling business.

"Herr Wening! Herr Nowak! Ich melde mich gehorsam!" Abo rattled at our next visit. "There is a man in the crew who calls in sick much too often. He's big and strong, and he doesn't look sick to me."

"And his name is?" Wening asked threateningly.

"Sapozhnik."

"Let's pay him a visit," Wening snapped to the chauffeur.

We found Ivan seated on a low stool in his cottage, repairing a shoe.

"So you're sick, are you?" Wening yelled. "You Ukrainian swine!" He kicked him, and the half-resoled shoe fell to the floor. "You saboteur! You partisan! Get out of here! We'll see what the police have to say!"

In the car, Ivan, scared by this unexpected crisis, begged me to translate his excuse and plead for him in German.

"It's all a mistake! I won't do it again," he begged. "I'm completely innocent!"

That last assertion offended Wening's sense of propriety.

"Innocent?" he roared. "You pig! That makes it fifty lashes instead of twenty!"

Ivan was so strong that he easily survived the punishment, administered to him by two Ukrainian policemen who were even worse brutes than he. Although hardly able to stand, he reported to Abo the morning after, ready to take up his shovel.

"Do you see that stump?" Abo pointed to a particularly large one. "Remove it! On the double!"

That was the last time Abo saw Ivan, nor did he shed a tear when he heard that Ivan had caught Pneumonia and died suddenly. We both could only hope that his suffering had been like that of some of the Jews he had murdered.

Around this time, Kreutzer hired another non-Polish-looking Pole as a foreman. Swarthy, with brown eyes and wavy black hair, the slim, happy-go-lucky newcomer was clearly anything but a Slav. I couldn't detect a Jew under his exotic complexion but it was my guess that Victor was a Polish gypsy. A clever black-marketeer who had arrived from Dnepropetrovsk, he was soon introduced to me by Abo. In fact, the two became buddies.

Father, meantime, handled life as best he could. He cooked, kept the room clean, remained strictly kosher, and to pass the time he reviewed his vast knowledge of the Talmud, so much of which he had in memory. He also kept track of the Jewish calendar, remembering almost every holy day as it came up.

"September 30 will be Rosh Hashanah of the year 5704," he said one day in the fall of 1943. "Yom Kippur will be celebrated on Saturday, October 10. When Yom Kippur falls on a Saturday, it is considered even holier. You should try not to work that day. God will bless you for it."

We couldn't stay away from work, but on Saturdays everyone would usually leave at two o'clock, so we would have several hours of the holy day left.

"We won't take advantage of Pekuach Nefesh to break the law on fasting," I said, on behalf of all three brothers. "Each of us will pocket whatever food he can get hold of, and we'll all have the evening meal together when the first star appears."

Father prayed for all of us on the first day of Rosh Hashanah as he would on the ten days of repentance which followed. On the first eve, we all had a meal of bread, butter and fruit. Then, seated on our two chairs and on father's and Wilo's beds, we silently intoned the heartrending Kol Nidre prayer. The holiest day in the Jewish year had begun.

We collected and saved food at breakfast and lunch the next day, and had an excuse ready, if anyone should ask why. "Too busy to eat now. We'll eat in the field we would say."

That afternoon, we gathered once more in father's room. We imagined ourselves to be in a corner in a basement in fifteenth-century Spain, and that we were Marranos, Catholics outwardly, but ardent Jews within.

The hours passed slowly as father silently recited all the prayers. As a good Jew, he knew them all by heart. Eventually the prayers were finished, and he ever so softly chanted the Neilah, the concluding prayer. In it a good Jew accepts the will and the judgment of God for his destiny in the New Year to come. He next chanted the Kaddish for all of his family members known to be dead, and for all of the multitudes of Jews murdered by the Nazis.

Then as we waited for the fast day to end, father went out to the yard and searched the sky for the evening star. After about a quarter of an hour, though it seemed longer, he re-entered the room and, breaking our rigid rule, whispered in Yiddish, "Kinderlach. Wir kennen yetzt essen." Children, we may now eat.

That evening was an emotional one, joyous, yet sad. When it ended and Abo and I left the house, we whispered to the dark sky of the southern Ukraine, "L'shanah habaah b'Yirushalaim." The age old hope of all Jews. "Next year, may we all be in Jerusalem."

⧺ ⧺ ⧺ ⧺ ⧺ ⧺

CHAPTER

10

In the Eye

of the Storm

THOSE OCTOBER DAYS were crystalline and sunny. The nights were crisp, and would leave frost on the windows for the sun to thaw in the morning. The underground news from the front was hopeful, and Wening and his German personnel were tense and irritable.

Without ever mentioning the deteriorating situation on all fronts, the Germans would let their alarm show through by talking nostalgically at the dinner table about their families and their homes which were now threatened by Allied raids, and about their unhappiness in Dolgin-zewo. "Why are we stuck in this God forsaken Bolshevik hell?" was the common refrain.

Since Gestapo men from Krivoi Rog were almost daily visitors to our boss, it was only on Saturday and Sunday that my brothers and I could breathe more freely, for those were the days when the secret police did not work. It was with apprehension, that I saw, one Saturday afternoon, the arrival and departure of a Gestapo limousine from the company's offices.

There is a Polish adage which says, "The cap is burning on the thief's head." Roughly it means, The guilty have reason to fear.

"Did that car have anything to do with me," I wondered. Though busy writing a report, I couldn't help but see that the officer entered the administration building with an envelope in his hand, and that he left without it.

I was one of the few in the company who worked on Saturday afternoons. Burdened with blueprints and progress reports as I was, I always had a lot of catching up to do on Saturdays. I knew that I would not be able to sleep that night unless I found out what was going on, and so I sneaked into Wening's office. There it lay on his desk, a neat Gestapo envelope with "Top Secret" stamped on it.

I took the envelope in my hand and examined it on all sides. "It might mean life or death for me" I thought.

As an old hand with documents, I knew I could open the envelope and reseal it so that no one would know it had been tampered with. I brought a little water to a boil on an alcohol burner, then carefully steamed the envelope open.

I was relieved to find that the contents had nothing to do with me. It was an order addressed to Wening. "On Monday, you will deliver, to the Gestapo headquarters in Krivoi Rog, your employee, the Jewess Wala, and her daughter." Their address followed.

Wala was one of Lida's co-workers in the warehouse. She was a local woman who looked so Ukrainian that no one, not even her neighbors, had any idea that she was Jewish. Not only that, but Paul, one of Wening's German employees, was her lover.

Obviously, I was faced with a dilemma. My first reaction was not to get involved. "Don't touch the shit. You might start smelling," was a saying every inhabitant of Lvov heard often. Then my thoughts turned to the many Jews who had been killed there. We were fewer alive each day, and it was clear to me that every person saved would help ensure the future generations of our people.

I thought of Rozia and of the magnificent Polish family that was sheltering her. Those Poles were putting their lives on the line to save a Jewish child. I had no right to do less.

I resealed the envelope and put it back where I had found it and returned to my office. There I arranged my papers in an orderly pile, so that no one would suspect that I'd left in a hurry. Then I dashed over to father's room.

When I arrived, I was breathless. I gasped at Wilo, "There is a mitzvah, a good deed, that you must perform." I gave him a slip of paper. "I've written down the address of a woman who is pretending to be Ukrainian. She's really Jewish. Run and warn her that the Gestapo is looking for her and her daughter. Tell her not to lose a minute but to get out! Don't mention my name—I must not be involved."

Monday morning it was business as usual, at first. Wening joined me, and together we inspected a couple of work sites. A little later the bomb dropped.

"Drive to this address," Wening ordered the chauffeur, handing him a piece of paper.

"Where are we going?" I asked innocently.

"To Wala's. Do you know her?"

I hesitated.

"Oh, yes! I think I do. Isn't she a woman who works in the warehouse?"

"She's a *Jewish sow*, that's what she is!" Wening was livid. "She has ruined my reputation with the Gestapo! I run a Judenrein, Jew-free, business! No Jewish pigs work for me!"

"We'll pick her up and send her to Krivoi Rog with that bitch of a daughter of hers. The Gestapo will settle her accounts. Such a swine—all the good I've done for her! I treated her like a *person*, and now it turns out she's a Jewess!"

The car stopped in front of Wala's small dilapidated old house. "You come with me!" Wening ordered. We ran up to the house. The door was open, and the place was a shambles. The woman had obviously fled.

"That sow!" Wening was sweating profusely. "What am I going to tell the Gestapo? I can't believe it! How did she know?"

My knees were weak. I tried to show anger and

dismay. I dutifully searched the house with him, looking under the bed and checking the covered potato pit. As I searched, I offered Wening some ideas. "Somebody must have tipped her off. She wouldn't just leave on her own. Maybe it was one of her German boyfriends?"

It was a cautious remark, not too explicit, and I watched for his reaction.

Wening sprung for it. He hit his forehead with the palm of his hand.

"Of course, her boyfriend Paul!" He glanced at me. "Nowak! You have just solved my problem. You nailed it! Now I know what to say to the Gestapo." As we left the house, I felt a wave of relief.

The fall saw the war heading in our direction. By the end of October, there were rumors that the Red Army had forced the Germans back and that the front line was now only 100 kilometers east of Dolginzewo. The southern Ukraine had been the breadbasket of the Soviet Union. Now it served the same role in Hitler's empire — that was one reason why the Wehrmacht defended its positions there so desperately.

We were anxious when we heard the distant rumble of heavy artillery. In November 1943, with the first snow falling, Russian bombers flew over these occupied territories.

The initial air raids were not very heavy. The planes flew very high to avoid the well-trained German antiaircraft gunners, and although it was clear that the depots and railway tracks were the targets, the bombs usually burst in empty fields. Occasionally, they would hit a peasant barn. Once a bomb fell on an army base, but as fate would have it, it exploded in a prisoner-of-war camp, killing and wounding many Russians and not scratching a single German. This was only the first inkling of the changes to come in the war. We almost loved being bombed by friendly fire. At night, the explosions and the hollow thunder of artillery were our lullabies.

Because some of the top railroad officials had moved to the northwest of Dolginzewo, we speculated that the front line must be much closer than officially admitted. Like hurricanes, the armies would approach our area, twisting and turning but moving in none-the-less.

I had become Wening's confidante on matters of war strategy. "I don't like it," he would say. "We're too close to the front. I'd like to liquidate our shop and move up north, before a Bolshevik bomb destroys everything."

What was really troubling him was the possibility of being captured by the Russians. The Germans had so devastated the Soviet Union, brutalizing and murdering millions of Soviet citizens, that they could hardly expect less from the Red Army. Wening complained aloud about why his business had to remain in its highly exposed location when other German companies were permitted to leave.

The focus of our construction activities nonetheless was shifted from Kaganowicze to Dolginzewo. Now, I could see Abo more often on my inspection tours. He, and Victor the Gypsy, who had become close friends, had their crews work next to each other, laying track and putting the depot in shape for the retreating German army to use.

One morning, toward the end of November, Wening's

managers and supervisors were called to an urgent meeting at the company's executive offices. Uncertain of what might be announced, the participants shared guesses and predictions. Everyone spoke under his breath, fearing bad news.

Wening stepped in, accompanied by Thiel, who was just about to leave on vacation. The owner quickly posted himself behind his desk and stood there, pale and distressed, staring past us.

He cleared his throat and started to speak. "Gentlemen!" he began. "Ladies and gentlemen!" he corrected himself, as there were a few female secretaries in the group. "I have some news which I must share with you. It is not very good news." He paused and wiped his forehead with a handkerchief. "The railroad district headquarters has just ordered me to put the company on alert. We must be prepared to relocate all personnel, equipment and supplies on very short notice. Each of you must be ready to board the company train when the order arrives. Have your most important possessions packed and ready." He paused again to mop his forehead. Then he concluded, haltingly, "This is all I have to say at this time, ladies and gentlemen. Thank you for your cooperation."

The remaining work in Kaganowicze was discontinued that day, and the Ukrainian laborers there were sent to Dolginzewo to help take down the prefabricated barracks that had been raised just a short time before. Entire wooden walls, roofs and other sections of buildings were put on flat trucks and dispatched for re-loading on freight trains.

This was when I began helping the chauffeur, Ivan. "If you can arrange for the partisans to steal a couple of trucks," I told him, "I'll make sure that they're loaded with some of the disassembled barracks. They might become the first housing in the reconquered areas. My contribution to the cause."

Thus two truckloads of building parts soon made a "detour" toward the Soviet-controlled sectors of the Ukraine.

The company evacuation train was organized according to usual Nazi rules. One car was reserved for Polish employees, another was set aside for a Mr. Demczyn, a Ukrainian engineer and an ardent Nazi collaborator, since he had a large family to take care of. The rest of the train was to be filled with Germans and the Ukrainian women some of them kept as mistresses.

We four Jews had two special problems. We would have liked to stay and be liberated by the Russians, but that would be dangerous. Nazi Security Police and the SS would most certainly arrive after the train had departed and comb the town for men. Our second problem was father. If we left him behind, the SS might find him and kill him; if he came with us, he would arouse the curiosity of everyone on the train.

"He'll come with us," I decided. "I'll come up with a story if anyone gets interested."

The problem wasn't solved easily. Father wouldn't hear of putting his sons in jeopardy. "You have already given me a gift of four months of decent life," he argued. "It has been like being born again. Now, if God calls me, I will heed His call." That he said was a proper attitude for an orthodox Jew — resigned acceptance.

"Sooner or later, we'll all die," I replied. "God has protected you so far because you had the will to fight for your life. It would be a sin to give in now. God wants you to continue fighting!" Pressured by the three of us, father finally accepted our plan.

A second concern was Abo's friend Victor. Although he had met each of us individually, he had never seen all of us under one roof for any length of time. He was clever, and might put two and two together and come up with four Polish Jews, traveling on a German train, under the Führer's unqualified protection.

Fortunately, Victor wasn't thinking about us. He was busy weaving romantic designs around the daughter of the collaborator Demczyn. He actually contrived to move into the engineer's private car and become a member of his household.

The preparations to leave took two days and two nights. On the morning of the third day, I went to Lida's house to pick up my few belongings.

She was standing out front as I arrived. Seeing me there, her aunt also came out to hear the latest news. She sensed that something was up, since it was unusual for me to show up in the middle of the day.

Lida listened intently as I explained. "I've got to leave. The company has gotten orders to move out. They wouldn't tell us where we're going. It's just that everyone, including all the Poles on the staff, has to leave Dolginzewo."

She was sorry to lose her boarder, but there was nothing she could do about it. She had grown accustomed to wartime changes. "I hope it won't be a long trip," I continued. "As a matter of fact, I hope we might even be liberated by the Russians. They say the Red Army is nearby."

"That's what everybody thinks," Lida said. "Maybe we'll be free soon and this nightmare will be over." With that, the two women bid me farewell, "God be with you!" Lida and I shook hands, but there was more than the normal expression of friendship in that gesture.

The dismantling of the barracks went on under the supervision of eternally drunken German foremen. Shaky and uncertain about the future, they drowned their frustrations in native schnapps and the local home brew.

My chauffeur, meanwhile, kept diverting truckloads of prefabricated housing to the advancing Soviets. The foremen couldn't care less at that point whether the barracks went west or east, they were preoccupied with saving themselves.

Thiel had left for Germany on his well-timed vacation, while Wening was busy outdrinking his staff and stripping local farmers of their foodstuffs. The scene was set for a full-scale evacuation.

On the fifth day after the staff meeting, the order arrived for Wening's staff to leave their work sites and board the train. Late that evening, the train was attached to a tender and a locomotive. Amid steam, smoke and a cloud of coal dust, the long succession of cars carrying some of the first German refugees chugged off slowly — in the wrong direction. Our train went south, the tracks west having been commandeered by the retreating army.

Hours later, as the sun rose beyond the small, barred

window of our car, father and I sat on the floor facing each other. Each of us had his own thoughts. Father was probably thinking of mother, while I tried to sort out what the latest developments meant to us.

The train came to a halt. Harsh German voices could be heard outside. It sounded like a bitter argument. It is a disturbing characteristic of the German language that words of endearment can sound like curses.

Someone pulled open the sliding door of our car. It gave me a start. Jews arriving in Nazi extermination camps also had the doors of their cars pulled open, and there were harsh German voices outside to order *them* to their deaths.

We weren't anywhere near the gas chambers, thank God! The train, sidetracked on a dead-end, rested placidly in the middle of nowhere while the engineer waited for his orders.

We had a quick meal, went outside and watched an endless line of trains heading northwest on other tracks. They were loaded with tanks, heavy guns, and tens of thousands of soldiers.

I walked over to Wening's private car, hoping to learn more about the situation from my boss. He was in no mood to talk, however; he was depressed, angry and very drunk.

That afternoon, our train moved once again. No one knew where it was going. Some guessed that we were heading toward Nikolayev, while others thought Odessa. When we stopped that night, we found out that we had entered the marshaling yards for the military at Apostolovo. We were again shunted to an off siding and temporarily forgotten.

The night was cold and clear. A full moon lit the huge

railroad yard. It was jammed with trains full of precious military equipment.

It started as an intermittent rumble from the east, at first barely audible. Then it got louder and louder. Search-lights went up, then anti-aircraft guns began firing. Russian airmen, still fearing the precision of Hitler's gunners, dropped their bombs from high up onto the desolate steppes of the Ukraine. Again, even an ineffective air raid was a tonic. We wanted to live of course, but had our train been hit that night we would have died joyously, knowing that so many of the Führer's followers would die with us.

The raid ended, and later that night screams were heard from Demczyn's car. It was his wife and daughter, running out of the car, yelling for medical help.

We ran toward them with a lot of others. There was no doctor on the train, but one of the army veterans had been a medic. He knelt next to Demczyn, lying on the floor of the car, and put an ear to the man's chest. Then he got up, turned to the bystanders and announced, "It must have been a heart attack. He was gone before anybody realized that he was sick. He never knew what hit him."

At dawn, Victor and another man from the Demczyn's household dug a grave at the edge of the railroad yard. The land Demczyn had betrayed in his life accepted him in his death. There was always room for one more on the great steppes of the Ukraine.

The train pulled out of the yard later that night and inched along, stopping every few minutes to let priority military trains pass. We hoped that we were heading someplace less dangerous.

In the morning, after switching tracks repeatedly, we

sped up a little in the direction of the south. It was maddening. Trains went past in the opposite direction. Some headed west in what seemed full-fledged escape; others, perhaps bound for the ultimate challenge, rushed east. Helpless and seemingly astray, we continued south, only to stop at last on a siding near Nikolayev.

From there we could see wave after wave of Soviet planes flying over, bombing the town mercilessly and leaving it in flames. Again we could hear artillery fire, this time relatively close by — whether from German or Russian guns, we had no idea. It made no difference in any case. All that counted was that the Russians were coming.

It continued on like this day after day. We were simply observers, waiting as crowded military trains passed us by carrying German troops and Ukrainian collaborators. Ukrainian policemen scrambled all over the tracks, along with the SS and German civilians — their wives and children.

Rations were reduced because of the rise in the number of evacuees. Finding enough food became a necessity, and some of the more daring passengers went foraging for edibles, among them Victor and Abo. A kolkhoz was found a few kilometers from where we were stopped — a communal farm — before Soviet rule it had been a Jewish settlement, and now under Nazi occupation it had been confiscated and run by Ukrainian Volksdeutsche. Everyone had fled in fear of the Red Army's retribution, leaving behind ample supplies of potatoes, other vegetables, grain and best of all, fowl.

Abo learned from Victor how to build a fire and cook on it. For days we feasted on delicious chickens, ducks and geese. Again, father abstained. He would have died from hunger rather than eat fowl butchered in a non-kosher way. To save him from starvation, we gave him thick vegetable soup, and we all gorged ourselves on summer fruit.

Though we were now eating well, I worried. "We're not only stagnating here, we're like sitting ducks," I said to the others. "Let's suppose the Gestapo suddenly decides to take a closer look at everyone on the train. We'd be finished! Or look at it from the opposite side, the Russians catch us and take us all prisoners. We'd be treated as collaborators — stood against the wall and shot."

Abo agreed. "Why don't we run away? We've been on the run since May anyway."

"Run with father?" I couldn't keep a trace of mockery from my voice. After so many months, Abo still had to learn the most basic facts of survival. But an idea came. "Instead of the four of us trying to escape, why not make the entire train go? That would look perfectly proper."

Abo snorted. "It sounds preposterous."

"I'll take it slowly," I explained. "I'll talk to Wening, sound him out and try to persuade him to send me on an errand back to Dolginzewo."

One end of the boss' private car had been turned into an office. He was sitting there behind his desk, reviewing unanswered correspondence, when I asked to speak with him.

"Sit down," he said. "What can I do for you?"

Hustling is not an easy business. I hesitated, recited a quick prayer to myself — the Shmah Yisroel, the ultimate invocation for a Jew facing death. Then I unfolded my plan.

"The official bulletins claim, Herr Wening, that we have fought off the Bolsheviks in the Krivoi Rog zone and are mounting a counter-offensive."

Wening nodded slowly. "That is correct."

"Am I to understand that the Dolginzewo area is still intact?"

A nod acknowledged the truth of this as well.

"We are sitting here, in all this mess, while we might be back there, saving what's left of your business."

Wening's opaque stare brightened. "And how do you propose we do that?" he asked anxiously.

I cleared my throat and said to myself, "Here goes!" "With an official safe-conduct from you in hand, I'll try to return to Dolginzewo. When I get there, I'll examine the situation and consult with the head of the railroad district administration. If it seems that the plan is feasible, I'll persuade him to order our train back. Although returning to Dolginzewo will, of course, help you save your own business, it will also be a patriotic act. It will become a symbol for other German companies to follow — an expression of confidence in the Führer."

The latter part of the speech was simply the icing. Wening was sold on the plan from the start of my spiel, and the flag-waving gave him a reason to take advantage of his chief engineer's chutzpa.

"You might have a point," he said with phony caution. "Yes, I'm inclined to go along with you. What the hell, let's do it!" he concluded, banging his fist on the desk as though it were the seal of approval. "We'll prepare a travel order for you, and may God and the Führer protect you."

He called in his private secretary and dictated a letter of request to "any authority concerned," military, SS, railroad or civilian, to extend every possible help and courtesy to his chief engineer and personal courier, Herr Stanislaw Nowak. He signed the letter, affixed the company seal, slipped it in an envelope and handed it over to me.

"You are a smart and courageous man, Nowak," he said.

We shook hands, two patriotic men hoping only to serve the Fatherland.

When I described the scene to my family, my brothers were speechless. My father grew somber, but he knew that my mind was made up. As a last precaution, we discussed the steps to take in case I did not return or if there were other problems. They would have to take care of themselves, and Abo would be in charge.

I left at first light. I presented Wening's letter to a military policeman and was allowed onto a troop train that was heading north, toward Krivoi Rog and Dolginzewo.

Dolginzewo wasn't the placid town it had been less than a month before. The streets were deserted. Signs were posted everywhere, ordinances announcing that this was a war zone and ordering all local men between the ages of fourteen and fifty away, under penalty of death. This was a precaution intended to help protect the German troops from sabotage by partisans.

The days were getting shorter, and to avoid being caught on the street after curfew I knocked at the door of the house nearest to Wening's headquarters. A woman opened the door.

"Mr. Nowak!" she exclaimed. She had been one of the company's Ukrainian employees. "What are you doing here? There isn't a single man left in town!"

"May I come in?"

"Of course." She locked the door behind me.

"I'm on official business. But first, tell me, how are things here?"

"Terrible. At first there was continuous bombing, then there was heavy gunfire. For a few hours we could even hear machine guns, but then it got quiet. I think the Russians must have been turned back. But the Vlasov brigade is stationed nearby, and their soldiers have raided the town a couple of times. The collaborators have thrown a dragnet over the entire region. They shoot men and boys on sight, or drag them to a detention camp, which is a death sentence anyway. Everyone who is able to has left. Men and boys are in hiding, who knows where."

"That is bad news. Because the company would like to return."

She gave me a tired smile.

"Maybe it would be good. Maybe, with the company here life will be easier."

"I have to get to Lida. I'll spend the night at her place, and first thing in the morning, I'll go to see the railroad administrator. He's the only one who has the power to give Wening permission for his train to return to Dolginzewo."

"You can't go to Lida's at this hour. You're a man. They'll shoot you." She thought a little. "Unless . . ." and she smiled impishly.

"Unless what?"

"Please don't laugh at me! I thought that if you shaved

- 173 -

your mustache and dressed as a woman, you might risk going out. I'll even walk you over to Lida's. It will be safer for two."

Under the circumstances, the idea seemed worth trying. Still, I noted, "I don't have a razor."

"I'll give you one of my husband's." She sighed. "Who knows where he is now?"

I shaved my face clean, though I cut myself in the process — the resulting scar stayed with me for years. Then I put on a woman's outfit. "Do you want to look in a mirror?" she said, laughing. I preferred not to. "Let's go," I said curtly.

Once again in disguise, I thought to myself, as my chaperone and I hurried along the darkened streets. I was bitter and somewhat amused at my predicament. I was a Jew, I was a Pole, I was a Ukrainian woman.

A German sentry made a pass at the two stray females. We giggled coquettishly. When we arrived at Lida's house, it was in total darkness. Lida, assuming a sentry, answered our knock without asking who was there.

"What can I do for you?" she said, startled to see two women. "May we come in?" I asked. Lida stared in confusion at the female who spoke with a man's voice. Then she recognized me.

"Mr. Nowak! Oh, my God!" She cried and laughed at the same time over this spectacle of her friend the engineer wearing an ample peasant skirt and a babushka.

"Come on! Stop laughing!" I was getting embarrassed. "Let me get into my room and change. I want to give this ridiculous disguise back to this nice woman."

The next morning, I walked undisturbed to the railroad headquarters. I crossed the tracks which, as always, were jammed with trains full of soldiers and military equipment.

The administrator and I had met before. "What are you doing here, Herr Nowak?" he said in lieu of a greeting. "This is no place for a civilian."

"In a way, I'm not a civilian. Not at the moment." I handed him the letter. "What do you wish me to do?" he asked after reading it.

"Herr Wening wants to contribute to the war effort in the best way he can. He requests your written order for the return of the Wening train to Dolginzewo."

The administrator whistled with admiration.

"Does this mean you will help us?" I asked.

"Our army has pushed the Russians back. Good times will return! What I'm trying to say is that I'll go through channels immediately and get your train back here as soon as possible."

The first half of my mission had ended successfully. Now I was faced with the trip back to Nikolayev, but I never had to take it. Two days after I got to Dolginzewo, the Wening train returned. I could see the relief, not only on my brothers' and father's faces, but on Wening's as well.

After a late dinner, we began moving our belongings discreetly back to our lodgings. Abo was to move in with father and Wilo, instead of going to the dormitory. But we slept on the train for several nights in order not to arouse suspicion, and finished moving in the meantime.

The situation was not promising. The Germans expected the Russians to advance shortly. All the Poles had gotten strict orders not to leave the vicinity of the train, in case we had to evacuate quickly.

No one noticed when father left the train on the third day. Since he did not work for Wening, he wasn't missed. The rest of us decided to hide in town when the train left. We were very uneasy about this move, however. When the order to leave came, we would simply disappear in different directions, returning to our old quarters after a reasonable time.

The order for everyone to return to the train reached us a week later. The three of us immediately set off. The next few hours were frightening. We wondered if the train would be held for us or if the local police had been sent out to find us. Fortunately, we weren't that important to the Germans, and the train left barely half an hour after notice was given. The Germans and the railroad management were concerned for themselves and little else.

We met at father's and celebrated our being together. We felt that we had a chance of being liberated. Still, our dreams of freedom were sobered by the new reality, we were alone, without income or a source of food, in a war zone. That night, Dolginzewo was a no-man's land.

⧗ ⧗ ⧗ ⧗ ⧗ ⧗

CHAPTER

11

In the Midst

of the German Army

O<small>UR EUPHORIA BECAUSE OF</small> escaping from the Wening refugee train could not last long. Without jobs, we were easy prey for the SS, the Wehrmacht and the Vlasov army that would soon flood into Dolginzewo. All we had in the way of food was a bag of potatoes and a few sacks of sunflower seeds — a meal for birds, not people. The seeds were useful in bargaining for other food, though. Seed, because of its cooking oil, was highly valued.

Nor could we stay indefinitely in father's room. There was little space there, and the landladies, the two widowed sisters, might suspect us of being undesirables. Should the Germans arrive, they might betray us as deserters.

I decided to stay with Lida. "It won't solve our problem," I said, "but it will reduce it by twenty-five percent."

Lida and her old aunt proved invaluable. "Let's go to work," Lida said. "Our basement has a dirt floor. We can dig a hole in it, and turn it into a hiding place."

The three of us worked with spades and shovels into the night. The final result was a fairly comfortable hideout, with an entrance behind a heap of potatoes which Lida had stockpiled for the long winter.

Typically for the Ukraine in December, snow covered the town and the barren fields around it. Communication between us was a problem, since neither Abo nor I dared show our faces outside. Martial law was again in effect, and men our age could be summarily executed. Wilo was the link between us. Though almost fourteen, he looked like a twelve-year-old. This helped protect him. He became our only source of news and rumors. We braced ourselves for the winter.

"We've eaten the last of the food," Wilo reported one day. "As of today, father, Abo and I are hungry."

"I can't abuse Lida's hospitality and take her potatoes," I replied. "They're her only food for the winter. But Abo and I can take a couple of sacks of sunflower seeds to the mill, and have them pressed for oil. With oil, we'll be able to barter for other food. In the meantime, take some of my bread and apples. They'll keep you alive for a while."

On December 29, 1943, Abo borrowed a sleigh from

the landladies and brought it over to Lida's house. He and I loaded it with two sacks of seeds and dragged it toward Krivoi Rog, the mill being midway between the towns.

Abo pulled the 120-pound load and I trudged behind, pushing. Although we wore warm clothing, the icy air penetrated to our bones. Snow flurries hit our faces in gusty whirls. The cold wind made it hard to breathe.

Visibility was poor. With horror I suddenly saw a soldier on a horse, riding slowly in our direction. He held the reins in his left hand, and in his right hand he cradled a carbine. It was not a propitious sight.

"What do we do?" moaned Abo. "If things get bad," I said, "hide in that lone house at the edge of the road. Go in the front door and run out the back if necessary. And forget about me!"

The rider was now almost on top of us. He was a Vlasov Cossack, wearing a heavy German coat and a tall sheepskin hat. A bandolier filled with cartridges was slung across his chest.

"Stop right there!" he ordered in a deep voice. There was no need for him to aim the carbine at us. I was sure he was able to shoot at point blank range. "Who are you?"

"Employees of the German Wening Construction Company in Dolginzewo," I said in German. "I'm an engineer. This one with me is a foreman."

Abo acted as interpreter, translating my German into Ukrainian.

The Cossack viewed us with suspicion.

"What are you hauling in those sacks?"

"Sunflower seeds. For the mill."

"Show me your papers!"

We produced our Wening documents. I was sure he didn't understand a word that was written on them, maybe he didn't even know how to read.

"What are you doing here? This territory is out of bounds for civilians!"

"We missed our evacuation train. We're stranded, and we need food."

"I don't know about that!" the Cossack boomed. "You'll have to come with me."

I winked at Abo, and he took one last desperate chance.

"I have to go to the toilet," he said.

The Cossack didn't understand. Abo tried the German colloquialism.

"Ich muss scheissen!"

Now he understood. "Make it fast," he ordered, pointing the carbine at the nearby hut.

He didn't have to repeat it. Abo went slowly toward the house, then around its far side, and finally, when he reached the back, he ran. That, I thought, was the last I would ever see of him.

Ten minutes passed. "Where's the other guy?" the Cossack asked.

"Ich verstehe nicht," I responded calmly in German. "I don't understand."

We waited for a few more minutes. Finally, out of patience, the Cossack rode over to the hut — making me follow.

"Where is the man who came here?" he asked the peasant woman who emerged from the house.

"What man? I haven't seen a man." She shook her head in confusion.

The Cossack cursed picturesquely in Russian. Then, frustrated, he turned his horse and, pointing his carbine at me, snapped in a universally understood tone of voice: "March!"

He rode on his mare and I, having abandoned the sled with the sunflower seeds, plodded behind. Soon, we ran into a couple of German guards who spoke simple Ukrainian.

"Who's this man in the leather jacket?" one of them asked.

"He claims he's a German who works in construction," the Cossack explained.

Within the hour, we arrived at what appeared to be a post manned by the German military and Vlasov Cossacks.

A local man examined my papers and interrogated me.

"I don't believe you missed the train," he concluded. "Do you want to know what I think? You're a spy."

He summoned two Ukrainian guards.

"Take this man to Krivoi Rog, to the Sonderdienst. Let them find out who he really is."

I felt a chill. The Sonderdienst was the bloodthirstiest commando group in the Gestapo. I was afraid that I had run out of luck. When, after a walk in hip-deep snow, I saw the prison walls with SS guards on top of them, I silently recited the Shmah Yisroel. This was the end, and I readied myself to face the Lord. I was back in a place which, although officially without Jews, felt like the Judenlager in Lvov to me.

I was thrown into a very large cell crowded with all sorts of prisoners, mostly Ukrainian men of various ages and backgrounds. The insulting title by which the guards addressed all inmates was "verfluchter partisaner," damned partisans.

As of now, I, too, was nothing but a damned partisan, though I stood out from the crowd because I was dressed in a neat leather jacket and sported my regrown blond mustache.

Late in the afternoon, two guards opened the cell door. While one handed a tin bowl and a slice of bread to each inmate, the other dipped a ladle into a pail and poured some watery soup into the bowls.

I put part of my ration of bread into a pocket; it is good to have a reserve supply of food, I thought. After eating, I walked around the cell, hoping to find a familiar face in the ragged crowd.

I had no luck. Like a white raven, I felt looked on with suspicion and hostility. Those men were partisans indeed, and I, well-groomed and German speaking, must have seemed like an enemy snitch to them. As though intent on making my position even more difficult, an SS guard yelled from the other side of the bars, "Hey, you! What are you doing surrounded by these pigs?" and to make matters worse, he threw me two cigarettes.

Wherever I turned, I met cold, expressionless eyes. I was surrounded by enemies outside the cell and inside. I decided, finally, to squat next to an old man. He smelled of dung and machorka, the strong Russian tobacco. My spot on the cement floor next to him seemed to be the safest. I tried to rest.

In the morning, weary from a practically sleepless night, my legs sore from my cramped position, I went to the opposite end of the cell. Two toilet barrels stood there, both filled to the brim with excrement and urine. A man dropped his pants and relieved himself on the floor. Another prisoner stepped into the feces and urinated in the general direction of the improvised latrine. Nauseated, I returned to my spot at the side of the old man.

A little later, two guards arrived.

"Aufstehen!" they yelled in German. "Get up!"

We lined up for roll call. My head itched. I scratched it, and a louse found its grave under my nail.

We were each given a slice of black bread and a ladleful of hot liquid which the guards called tea. All day, about once every hour, the door would open and a couple of new prisoners would be shoved in. Late in the afternoon, as the last group of new arrivals came in, I recognized one of them. It was Abo! Until then, I had hoped fervently that he had escaped the dragnet. I say I recognized him, though he was so bruised, pale and unkempt it was hard to do so. I was glad I'd saved a piece of my bread; he was famished, and ate it voraciously.

Abo's arrival improved my standing with the other inmates. A suspicious Volksdeutscher who hugged, fed and consoled a Polish teenager couldn't be all that bad.

Abo told me his story quickly. After escaping past the back of the hut he made his way to town and to father and

Wilo. They discussed my capture that evening, and in the morning Abo decided to act. Taking father's silver cigarette case with him — the last valuable we owned — he hoped to bribe the police. He arrived at police headquarters and introduced himself as a railroad employee, and asked to see the German police officer.

The effort was doomed from the beginning, since the area was off limits to men of his age. The Ukrainian Schutzpolizei put Abo under arrest immediately, and while searching him found the cigarette case. He had taken it. Abo had struggled and in the ensuing fight was badly beaten. A German officer who heard the tumult came in, listened to Abo's explanation and, strangely enough, gave the cigarette case back to him. At the same time, dissatisfied with Abo's cover story, he ordered him transferred to the detention camp at Krivoi Rog.

Although our situation was desperate, I was very proud of my brother's courage. He had risked his life for me.

An hour later, a group of SS officers arrived at the prison. They stood in the courtyard and discusssed our fate. Finally, one of them turned to the guards. I was straining my ears, and not one word escaped me. I was the only inmate who understood German and knew for sure what was in store for us.

"Put them on the train. They'll go to the front line, to the vicinity of Kherson. They can dig trenches for the Waffen SS. After that . . . nach dem Gebrauch, wir werden die Schweine umbringen! After we've used them, we'll kill the pigs!"

A Ukrainian interpreter in an SS uniform brought a bullhorn to his mouth. "Attention, prisoners! You will soon be marched to the train, which will take you to a labor camp," he lied. "You will proceed in orderly fashion and will strictly obey any commands. Any breach of rules, or any attempt to escape, will be punished with instant death."

A field kitchen arrived. Soup made of potato peels was distributed, and a slice of sodden black bread was handed to each of us.

As night fell, the order came to leave the cell. "Alle 'raus!" a harsh and impatient voice commanded. "Everybody out!"

"Right face! Forward march!"

Though exhausted, we reacted as a horse does to spurs. We marched to a nearby railroad siding. There, a freight train waited with three cattle cars that had been transformed into our cells, each had one barred air hole. A machine gun was mounted on top of the last car. We were ordered into the middle car. The sliding door was pushed closed, locked and bolted from the outside. There was a jolt from the front of the train. A tender and locomotive were being coupled to the front. There was another jolt and the cattle train moved. It was cold and completely black, that night of December 30, 1943.

I sat on the floor next to my brother. Although wrapped in a thin blanket which some good soul in the boxcar had lent to him, he was shivering from the cold.

"We've got to make a run for it," I whispered. He looked questioningly at the barred window.

"How?"

It was clear that we needed partners. I looked around. Partisans or not, most of the prisoners looked defeated; I couldn't count on them. Then a burly, bearded man caught my eye, and I turned to him.

"Listen, comrade," I said in Ukrainian. "You might not know it, but the Germans are going to shoot us."

He stared at me without saying a word.

"Don't pay attention to that guy!" someone piped up. "He's full of shit. We're going to a labor camp." Several others seconded him.

"You idiots! You believed the interpreter. He lied to you! I understand German. Believe me, if we don't run now, we won't be alive tomorrow."

There was an uproar at this. "What did the Germans say?" someone asked.

"They'll make us dig trenches and a ditch for ourselves. Then they'll shoot us."

The car fell silent. No one moved. Suddenly, the silent giant stood up, walked to the air hole, grabbed the bars and pulled on them. Nothing happened.

He turned to the crowd and searched it with his eyes. Then, pointing to four young men who still seemed to have some strength left, he ordered, "You! You! You! And you!"

They all stood up.

"Now, lift me!" he commanded. "Use me as a battering ram. Swing me so I hit the bars with my boots. Do it as many times as you have to. Don't stop until the bars break away."

We watched the way people watch at a circus.

Each of us held his breath as the four rammed the

huge Ukrainian at the bars, as though he were a log. At the fifth ram, the bars yielded. At the sixth, they broke away. The giant, now on his own feet, easily pulled out the remaining rods. The way was open, to freedom or to death by machine gun.

"I'm going first," the giant announced. That was his prerogative. No one argued.

"I'll go after him," I said to Abo. "And you follow me." I looked into his eyes. "If they shoot us, at least we'll die together."

He didn't reply. He was almost frozen with fear.

The first man was already through, and two more were lined up in front of the window. I joined them, praying that Abo would snap out of it and follow me.

My turn arrived. I climbed up with the help of two prisoners, slid my legs through the narrow window, commended myself to the Lord and jumped. It took a split second. My knee hit a section of extra rail that was lying along the track bed, a replacement in case of sabotage. My hand hit the icy ground and was cut open. Numb from the fall and bloody, I lay face down and waited for the sound of shooting. There was none. Soon there was no train either, only dark, stillness and fear of the unknown.

With difficulty, I got up. I hurt all over, but elation over escaping soon numbed the pain. I bound the cut in my hand with a handkerchief, then limped along the track. I hoped that the rest of the night might hold more good news, namely that Abo was somewhere nearby, waiting for me.

I walked for several kilometers. Now and then I called, "Piotr!" but heard not even an echo.

All at once a tall figure stepped out from the bushes. He was one of the four who had hurled the Ukrainian against the barred window. "Have you seen Piotr?" I asked anxiously. "The young man who was traveling with me?" "The last I saw of him, he was still in the car. He wasn't sure if he should jump."

Together, we dragged ourselves through the night. Occasionally I called out for my brother, though less and less frequently.

Two other escapees joined us. Both gave the same response. Piotr Siminski had not left the train.

At dawn, we reached a railroad crossing and a dispatcher's shack next to it. One of my companions went in. We were lucky, as the railroad man there hated the Germans.

"You're near Kazanka," he said as he came out to see the rest of us. "It's a small town — nothing important there, except a large Wehrmacht depot. Make sure, though, that you don't turn south. There's an SS company in that direction, just a few kilometers from here."

Yet another runaway from the prison train appeared. Another half an hour's walk, and the five of us limped into the outskirts of Kazanka.

"This is where we split up," the tall man said. "A bunch like us will cause suspicion. We'll enter the town one by one, and make sure we all head in different directions." He spoke with authority. He must have been a seasoned partisan, and we followed his instructions precisely.

I thought I'd clean myself up before going any farther. I stopped by a brook and, despite the cold, undressed and took a quick wash. I examined my swollen knee, rebandaged my hand and got dressed. It was tough to put on my boots. My feet were swollen and blistered from the long hike. Finally, I entered the town.

Kazanka was like Dolginzewo, a long main road lined with small houses and several crooked, ill-kept side streets. But, alas, there was no Lida there to offer me shelter. Dejected, I trudged down the road. A peasant woman was walking in my direction.

"Mother"—I addressed her in the Ukrainian fashion—"can you tell me where the nearest crossroad is?"

"Go straight ahead until you reach the German warehouse," she replied.

As I walked, I wondered: Abo had remained on the death train, I knew nothing of father and Wilo. Had they been caught and killed? And what about mother in the Judenlager? How could she survive? Once again I prayed—hoping for her survival. I had some greater hope for Rozia. The Prachtels are taking care of her. Our troubles were so great that I almost wanted to give up the struggle.

Then, I saw the Wehrmacht depot. It looked so much like the Wening compound in Dolginzewo that, in a way, I felt comforted. My despair eased. I went straight to a noncom who was standing in front of the barracks.

I greeted him in German. "Good morning! I can hardly tell you how glad I am to see you."

He stared at me. "Do I know you?"

"No, you don't." I smiled faintly. "But I'm sure you can help me."

I recounted the true part of my story. I was the

Wening Construction Company chief engineer. I had become separated from their refugee train because of a bad railroad accident. I didn't have to elaborate, since I knew he would ascribe my misfortune to the Russian partisans. I didn't forget to mention that I was Volksdeutsch. If he wanted to ask Wening for verification, it would only make my position more solid.

The sergeant, as it turned out, wasn't the least bit interested in verification. "You're a mess," he announced. "What you need now is a solid meal and a lift to Novyj Bug, the town with the nearest Wehrmacht headquarters."

He asked me to follow him to the warehouse, where he fixed a small bundle of cans of meat and soup and wrote out a permit allowing me to hop a ride on a military vehicle. "Have a nice trip," he said. "I hope you find your company train."

I ate quickly, then hitched a ride on a military truck. It was a long, uncomfortable ride on a bumpy road in the depth of the Ukrainian winter. The open truck had a tarpaulin cover that flapped in the wind, allowing huge blasts of cold air to hit me. The others were all German soldiers who slept most of the time. When they were awake, they weren't interested in sharing their feelings about the war that had begun four years before as a Blitz and that was supposed to end victoriously within weeks. The trip with all its stops was a long one.

It was getting dark as we reached Novyj Bug. The driver dropped me in front of the Quartieramt, the Wehrmacht's housing office.

The officer in charge was tipsy. It was December 31,

and his New Year's celebration had begun. Without asking who I was, he stopped me at the door.

"We're closed! We'll be open on January 2, 1944!" He slobbered. "How do you like that? Nineteen forty-four! September 1, 1939 seems like only yesterday!" That, of course, had been the official beginning of World War II.

"There isn't much I can do for you right now about a lodging referral," he went on. "What can I say? Knock at one house after another until someone agrees to take you in. Well, have a happy New Year. You, and the Fatherland and the Führer!" He pushed me out and locked the door.

It took a lot of knocking on doors. One after another, Ukrainian residents would say — no space available, and that their homes were crowded, or that they already had German tenants. Finally, late in the evening, I found a good samaritan.

"I have a vacant room with one bed," a well-dressed, middle-aged woman said, after opening the door for me. It was the nicest-looking house I had seen in the southern Ukraine. Furnished with taste, it even had a piano in the drawing room.

"You have a beautiful place here," I said.

"It's home," she replied modestly. "I have a boarder, a German civil engineer, but he's been gone for several days, and he did not tell me where. May I offer you a glass of tea?"

"Yes, thank you." She set the table, and together we had tea with bread and jam.

"You speak with an accent," she said.

"Yes. I'm a Pole from Lvov. And like your boarder, I'm

an engineer — the chief engineer with a railroad construction company. As our train was leaving Dolginzewo, the partisans blew up part of the track. I was caught in the bombing, injured, and before I knew it the train had pulled away without me. After that, I walked for miles before I could catch a ride. It was miserable. That's why I look like a bum. I don't even have money to pay you for the room, but I'll do so once I've caught up with my boss."

"Don't worry about that. I must say that you are fortunate. There's a Wehrmacht field hospital within walking distance, and you can go there, first thing in the morning."

"Oh, I will!" I felt uneasy at the thought, but she might grow suspicious if I refused. "Do you live all alone in this big house?"

"No, I have a twenty-year-old daughter. She has a good job, but her hours are long. She's almost never at home. She works as a secretary to the German district governor."

That reminded me of the district governor's secretary in Dnepropetrovsk. I still owed her a pair or two of silk stockings. I glanced once more at the fine furniture. The governor must have had a hand in decorating the house, no doubt as an act of fatherly kindness toward his young secretary.

By now, I was sore all over and had chills.

"Will you excuse me? I don't feel very well," I apologized.

"Of course. Try to get some sleep. Good night, and a happy New Year."

I dozed off, woke up and dozed again. I was feverish, and had nightmares.

Shouts in German woke me before dawn. No, it wasn't shouting. It was singing! A male and a female voice in awful harmony were croaking the German students' drinking song, "Trink! Trink Brüderlein! Trink!" Someone opened the door to my room, and an SS officer appeared with a young woman, both embracing, singing, and both obviously drunk.

The officer pointed angrily at me. "Who's that man? What's he doing in your bed?"

"That isn't my bed." Clearly, this was the landlady's daughter. How could she know what I was doing in her house?

"I'm the new boarder," I said in German. "Happy New Year to you, Herr Sturmführer! Have you got a cigarette to spare? And, maybe, a beer? I was wounded, you see, a few hours before the old year ended."

"I'll be right back," he promised. He left the girl and returned in a minute, bringing a glass of beer, a few cigarettes and some homemade cookies. "Enjoy! Here's to the Führer! And a happy New Year to you."

I joined in the toast and, after the pair left, fell into an uneasy sleep.

I woke up late, aching more than ever. My face was burning. A painful swelling had taken hold in my right arm — infection from the cut in my hand. I felt shaky and nauseated.

The landlady knocked on the door and brought me a glass of tea with honey. "You look very sick," she said, touching my forehead. "You should go to the hospital immediately."

"I don't have the strength," I complained. "All I want to do is sleep."

"Sleeping won't help, the hospital will. I'll send my daughter to find out when the emergency room opens."

I knew she was right, SS or no SS. She brought me a razor, I shaved, washed and started dressing.

The landlady returned, looking worried. "The hospital is closed until tomorrow morning," she said, "except for very badly wounded soldiers. I guess I'll have to take care of you until then."

She brought some alcohol and washed the cut. Wow that hurt! Then she dressed the wound with a clean bandage. "I'm going out with my daughter now, to visit relatives. But I'll be back soon," she promised.

I sat next to the window and for a while watched the traffic in the street. It swarmed with soldiers, cars, trucks, armored vehicles and heavy tanks. Occasionally, I could hear a low-flying airplane.

Weak with fever, I returned to bed and fell asleep. Subdued voices in the adjoining room woke me up. The landlady entered with a woman who turned out to be her sister-in-law, and once more put her hand against my forehead.

"You have a high fever. You need a doctor badly."

"I heard about your accident," the other woman added. "May this terrible war come to an end soon! My husband was drafted by the Red Army at the beginning of the fighting. I haven't heard from him since. I hope he's still alive."

I thought about Lida and her husband. Millions of Russian families had lost their fathers, brothers and sons. Just like the Jews. But their women were still alive, and so were their children. And when their men died, they usually fell with a gun in hand.

"I'll bring a bite to eat," said the landlady.

We ate in my room, drank tea and discussed the latest news.

"You look like a nice person," the sister-in-law said, smiling shyly. "Are you a Nazi?"

"No Nazi." I grinned back. "I hate them." It was a risky thing to say.

"Oh!" She sighed with relief. "Do you know what those monsters have done now? There was a train filled with prisoners coming from Krivoi Rog. When it stopped the guards discovered that some of the men had escaped. So what did they do? They stood all the prisoners who were left up against a wall and machine-gunned them. Right next to the railway station. May God curse them!"

At this, the room began to spin before my eyes. All my efforts had come to naught. Abo was dead, and I had no will to live any longer.

The women left me alone. They said I was very pale. I felt like death itself.

Early on January 2, the landlady forced me out. "Go to the hospital!" she commanded. "They can save you. If you stay in bed, you will get blood poisoning."

I forced myself to walk to the clinic, caring very little what happened to me at that point. If they discovered that I was a Jew, so be it. They couldn't hurt me more than they already had. I showed my railroad work card to the guard at the gate and he let me in. A long line of German soldiers waited at a door where a sign read Verbandplatz — dressing station. My leather jacket marked me as the only civilian there.

While I waited my turn, medics occasionally brought in stretchers with badly wounded soldiers on them. I was close to the head of the line when a stretcher passed by carried by two soldiers, with a third holding up a bottle of plasma. I glanced at the patient's face and got a jolt. Was I hallucinating from the fever, or was the wounded soldier Abo?

He recognized me too, as our eyes met for an eternal second of joy and silent communication. Then the soldiers carried him in.

My turn arrived. The long clinic room was divided into small cubicles, with a doctor and two nurses working in each. An enormous hospital ward was located beyond the far wall. That was where Abo would be transferred after he had been treated.

I entered the nearest cubicle. A physician examined me and gave me an injection. The nurses cleaned and dressed my hand, gave me a bandage to use the following day, and dismissed me. I didn't even have a chance to show them my swollen knee. To them, I was a relatively healthy specimen.

Between the injection and the knowledge that my brother was alive, I was feeling greatly improved. As casually as I could, I walked through the clinic instead of leaving it. When I saw Abo, I stopped and watched from a distance. His doctor and nurses finished with him, and two medics carried him on his stretcher into the ward. I followed. They placed him on an adjustable bed — one for orthopedic cases I supposed — hung a bottle of fluid on a pole, and placed a tube from the bottle to a vein in his arm. Then they left him alone.

I pulled up a chair and sat at his bedside. "Piotr!" I choked with emotion, then caught myself. "Mr. Piotr Siminski? The last time we saw each other, there was nothing wrong with you."

He squeezed my hand, conveying both joy at seeing me and his pain and apprehension. His bandaged foot was elevated, and someone had written on the chart hanging from one end of the bed, "Piotr Siminski. Soldat. Schwer verwundet." A badly wounded soldier.

What an uncanny twist this was. Next to his bed, some charitable hand had left a package for Piotr — ein Führer Paket, the Christmas present that each German soldier on the eastern front received from Hitler himself. The box was filled with chocolates, cigarettes and small packages of choice food from France, Belgium, Denmark and Holland. Even if it was only for a short while, my younger brother had it made. I remained a humble Volksdeutscher, but Abo had been promoted to Übermensch, a full-blooded German.

The anesthetic started to show its effect. Abo became groggy and fell asleep. I left without learning how my brother had ended up in a military hospital as a seriously wounded member of the Wehrmacht. Until then, I had thought that million to one encounters like ours happened only in novels. Now I knew better. Fiction couldn't compete with life.

"I was worried about you," my landlady exclaimed as I

entered her house. "It took you such a long time! Five hours! I was afraid they might have kept you in the hospital."

"No. There were just too many soldiers who needed attention before me. I got a shot of something, they dressed my cut, and now I feel much better."

"Are you hungry?" I admitted that I was, and just like a good Jewish mother, the Ukrainian woman brought me a bowl of chicken soup with vegetables.

It was time to plan my next move. I still had to learn exactly what had happened to Abo, and see how we could team up again. To that end, I paid him a visit the next morning. We spoke in whispers, using the coded language that we had developed during the past months. Even with that precaution, he couldn't tell me all of his story. There were too many strangers in the ward.

"The two of you look like brothers," said the soldier in the next bed.

"Thank you." I pretended the remark was a compliment. "We're from the same village in Silesia. I knew him when he was a little boy — actually, we're as close as brothers."

The panic button had been pushed for me. I couldn't be a daily visitor in the hospital ward. Our old rule of physical separation had to be brought back.

"So, when do I see you again?" Abo asked me as I was getting ready to leave.

"I've got to find a permanent place to live. I'll be back as soon as I have a new address."

I didn't want to overstay my welcome where I was

living. Besides, the other boarder might return, and there was always the little matter of the landlady's daughter and her SS boyfriend. I paid a return visit to the Wehrmacht housing office.

The same officer who had shut the door in my face on New Year's Eve was at his desk. As tipsy as he'd been three nights before, he recognized me immediately. It must have been my leather jacket.

"Welcome! Did you find a room for yourself?"

"I did. But I have more problems than housing. I'm an experienced highway engineer, separated from my unit all because of those damned partisans. Now I'm wounded and stranded and need a job if I want to eat. Can you help me? I think the Fatherland can use my skills." I showed him my documents from the Wening Construction Company.

"This damned Russian front!" the officer said. "Look at you! This is what's happening here to decent people! Let me call someone I know."

He picked up the phone and gave the operator a number. When the call went through, he gave someone at the other end a short description of my predicament, then passed the receiver to me.

"I understand you know how to build roads?" the voice at the other end said.

"I do. Roads, track beds. I know how to lay rails. I was the chief engineer for Wening in Dolginzewo, and the verfluchte partisaner blew up the tracks just as I was in the process of inspecting a site. I wound up stranded and in the Wehrmacht hospital."

"I'm sure we can use you here. We're a Wehrmact

engineering unit, Pioneer Park Company 21. We build and repair roads. Can you start tomorrow?"

"How far are you from here?"

"Not far at all. We're at the outskirts of Novyj Bug."

"I'll be there."

"Let me talk to the housing officer again," the voice said.

I returned the phone to my host. He marked something down on a pad and barked "Heil Hitler!" into the receiver.

"I'll fill out the Wehrmacht form for you," he offered. "Tomorrow, you can go to P.P. Company 21."

And that was how I got a job with the German army.

"I'll be leaving you tomorrow," I told my landlady later in the day. "I was lucky enough to locate my old unit, so I'll be joining them soon." Even though she was friendly, I didn't want her to know my new whereabouts. Thoughts of her daughter's boyfriend made me cautious.

The next morning, after a hearty breakfast, I left the house. I still had no money, and my only repayment for the landlady's kindness was a sincere "Thank you." Then I walked across town and a few kilometers down the road. In no time I reached the barracks of Pioneer Park Company 21.

I showed my Wehrmacht referral slip to the sentry at the gate, and he directed me to the office. Inside, I found a lieutenant and a non-com. "My name is Nowak," I said.

"Herr Nowak!" The lieutenant, a man with short-cropped hair and eyeglasses, pointed to a chair in front of his desk. I took a seat. "Your documents!" I handed him the referral form and my Wening papers. I recognized his voice; he was the one I'd spoken to on the telephone.

"I understand that you are Volksdeutsch?"

"On my mother's side."

"So you're as good as half a German." Was that a joke? He smiled politely and shook my hand. The ice was broken. "I myself am from Berlin. An old Nazi."

"That's nice. When do I start working? I want to do my part for the Fatherland once again."

"I like your attitude. Very positive. You'll join the company as of now. You'll get your uniform and your work kit, and we must find you a place to live. I want you quartered in a private home as close to the base as possible. You will have your meals in the mess hall, along with the non-coms and the soldiers. Sergeant!"

His aide snapped to attention.

"Show Herr Nowak around. Take him to the field, so that he can see various groups at work. Then assign him a lodging." He glanced back at me. "Where's your baggage?"

"I have none. Everything was left behind in Dolgin-zewo."

"Sergeant! Get a uniform for Herr Nowak, a couple of sets of underwear, socks, anything he needs. Immediately!"

As we walked toward the work sites, I inquired about other members of the unit. "Mainly older men," the sergeant said, "and wounded veterans. Some of them are still recuperating; this is considered light duty. Every morning, after the roll call, the ten heads of the kolkhozes nearby

Novyj Bug report to the base with all able-bodied peasant men and women. Then we divide them into two or more groups, as needed — this morning, we had only two groups — and dispatch them under military-police escort to the work sites. They fix roads, build new ones, do all sorts of manual work."

"Are they paid?"

He looked at me as though I had come from another planet.

"Paid? They are pigs! Pigs and slaves! They get their bread and soup at noon, that's all."

That afternoon, dressed in German army fatigues, I had my first Wehrmacht meal at a long table in the mess hall with soldiers and civilians from all over Germany. They spoke to each other in many dialects and laced their speech with scores of profanities. Nobody paid any attention to me. They were used to disease, death and transfers.

I looked younger than the others. My neighbor at the table began to talk to me. His mouth was full of food as he asked me my name.

"I'm Nowak," I replied. I avoided saying "Stanislaw," as that would have betrayed me as a Pole. I wanted to appear German to these people. Used to regional accents back home, they might not take me for a foreigner unless I made it obvious. "And where are you from?" I asked him.

"I'm from Vienna. The fellow on your left is from Munich. And you?"

"From Stratin, in Silesia."

With that, our conversation was over. I listened as he chewed noisily on his bread. When he turned his attention to the soup, he made a sound like water running down a drain. Most of the people around the table ate the way my neighbor did, and they called the Ukrainians pigs!

After eating, I reported back to the lieutenant. Along with my new Wehrmacht I.D., complete with a photograph and a seal, he gave me a few bits of advice.

"Roll call is at seven in the morning. Tomorrow, you'll join a group headed by another engineer, so you can get used to the way we operate. The day after, you'll have your own crew of peasants. And stay away from the local girls, they have V.D. Also, be careful with whom you speak. The place is filled with partisans and spies."

The sergeant had described the lieutenant at some length, and so I knew that I was dealing with a fervent Nazi, an ex-member of the Hitler Youth. The entire company, soldiers and civilians alike, despised him. Playing it by the book, I clicked my heels, raised my arm, shot a "Heil Hitler!" at him and marched out the way a good Nazi soldier should.

I went to look at the living quarters the sergeant had found for me — in a thatched-roof hut consisting of a large room which served as a kitchen, dining and bed room for the family of five. Off to a side there was a small room for me. This was a luxury under the circumstances.

My new landlords were extremely poor people. They were a middle-aged couple with two small children and a babushka, a toothless grandmother. Their clothing was covered with patches. They were so poor that they shared one pair of boots among themselves. Only one could leave the house at a time during the cold weather. The man of the house, forced to work all day for the army, was the primary user of the boots. When he came back from work early in the evening, his wife would put them on and go out to the forest to collect dry wood for the stove. During the day, the hut usually remained cold and the family hungry. Their official rations were extremely skimpy, and this was where I could be of help. Like a daily Father Christmas, I'd bring them anything edible I could lay my hands on. I soon became "Uncle Nowak" to the children, a title I came to savor. It made it easier to bear separation from father, Wilo and Abo.

My job was simple. All I had to do was supervise the local hands and show them the holes in the road to be filled with sand and gravel. I also functioned, as I had at Wening's, as an interpreter between the Ukrainian laborers and the German foremen.

At the end of the first week, on Saturday afternoon, I returned to the Wehrmacht hospital to see Abo and give him my new address.

By then, he was able to sit up in bed and to walk a little. Considering everything, he seemed to be in good shape.

"As soon as walking doesn't tire me out so easily, I'll be released from the hospital," he said. "The doctor says that might be in about two days."

He wanted to know about my army fatigues, and I told him briefly their story. As always, we had to whisper for fear of being overheard.

"I have something to tell you too," he said, looking shyly at the floor. "The army chaplain here has asked me to help him in his spiritual work with dying soldiers."

"You?" I couldn't believe my ears. Abo, the second son of a Hasid, was being asked to become some sort of an acolyte. "Why you? Out of all the choices, why did he have to give you the honor of burying the scum of the earth?"

"I wondered myself," Abo answered, showing a trace of amusement. "The chaplain visited me several times a day. All the while, he prayed for my health. He might have sensed that I'm deeply religious. You know what father always says when I pray: "Abo! You finish your prayers so quickly that I think you must know them all by heart! It's a good sign!"

He must have felt better if he could joke about himself, and thus my mood improved as well.

"Kidding aside," Abo continued, "the chaplain has a really keen interest in me. Maybe he believes he can save my soul. Or maybe he feels sorry for me, and doesn't want me to go back to the front. I told him that my family seldom went to church so — imagine! I'm learning the appropriate prayers and hymns. The chaplain coaches me — I think he even likes my voice. I don't mind the singing myself, it means I'm about to bury another murderer."

"We've both been blessed by God to have this opportunity," I said. "You, a Jew, burying Germans with a song. And I bury their tanks and armored trucks in the roads. I've been filling those huge potholes with a mixture of sand and lime. It gets as solid as granite in this cold, but by the end of March it'll be melting under them. My gift to them will be a quagmire."

Abo did not share my enthusiasm totally. Something had been troubling him, and he needed support.

"I'm not sure how long I'll be able to keep this up. It's

been difficult for me," he admitted. "After I bury the bastards, I can't sleep at night. I have nightmares about the dead and the dying. I re-live the last two years over and over again."

"I'm sorry it affects you so badly," I said, trying to give him some of my own inner strength. "I'm sure you'll get used to the job. In the meantime, try to block out the memories. Just think that the bodies you're burying are those of our worst enemies."

I still had to learn how he had survived the train. The hospital was hardly the place to talk about it.

I gave him direction to my Wehrmacht unit. "As soon as you're free to go, come and see me. Then we'll talk some more."

A few days later, Abo came to my work site. During lunch, we sat alone in an abandoned shack and I finally heard his tale.

"At first," he said, "I was afraid to jump out of the train. But then, several others did, and I didn't hear any shooting, so I screwed up my courage and jumped. I landed on the stones in the track bed; any farther away, and I'd have rolled down into the river.

"I was stunned, and when I had rested awhile I knew that one of my legs was broken. It was a really nasty fracture, too; there was a deep cut, and I couldn't stop the bleeding. And it hurt like hell. But I had to get out of there. Can you imagine crawling all night long? While bleeding? Well, that's what I did, hoping all the time that someone would find me and give me some help. Sure enough, at dawn I crawled right into a truckful of Wehrmacht guys. They wanted to know who I was, so I told them that I was a Polish Volksdeutsch foreman with Wening and an Organization Todt man. I told them I'd fallen off an evacuation truck. That's how I got myself checked in to the military hospital as a wounded soldier. I lost a lot of blood, and had a number of transfusions, so you are now talking to a man in whose veins flows the purest Aryan blood." He had acquired a sense of humor.

"And how's the job with the chaplain?"

"For the time being it is a job which I will have to do. I am assisting the chaplain with his burial duties."

"When soldiers die, I help dig graves for them. I think about the mass graves that Jews were forced to dig for themselves, before being shot, and I can't feel sorry for them. They brought hell on themselves, on the Jews, on everyone! I'll keep helping the chaplain. Maybe I'm destined to bury what's left of Hitler's army. May God strengthen me for my work."

Sunshine

Through the Rain

U NTIL MY ASSOCIATION with Pioneer Park Company 21, I had been under the impression that all Germans were confused. I had supposed that they had yielded to the fear of persecution by Hitler's brutal gangs, closed their eyes, stopped up their ears and refused to accept what was happening. Wasn't it, after all, a daily hope of all Jews in the ghetto or in concentration camps to see the Gestapo and the SS leave and the Wehrmacht, the regular German army, take over? It was thought, wrongly, that they were more civilized.

I learned that there was a fallacy in this reasoning and no basis for such assumptions. The time I spent with the Wehrmacht made me see the average German the way he really was, an arrogant "superman" hiding in the body of a simple burgher or a lowly peasant. Czechs, Poles and Ukrainians were objects of derision and contempt. Jews were an abomination, a blemish on the otherwise spotless coat of the Aryan world. One that could only be cleansed with blood and fire.

Their aversion to Jews found an outlet in dinner time conversation. An Austrian corporal who had been a street-car engineer recalled with pleasure an experience he'd had as he lay wounded in the military hospital of Lvov.

"Two Ukrainian policemen had caught a black-marketeering Jewess with a carton of butter. As they marched her to the SS headquarters, I had a brainstorm. My buddies and I were sitting in our wheelchairs in the courtyard when we saw the police pass by with her. 'Hey, you!' I shouted. 'Hold it! I want to help the bitch!'

"They stopped, and I said to the Jewess, 'Open up the butter!' She did. 'Eat the butter!' I ordered. She didn't protest, she just bit into one of the bricks. It must have been kosher butter, or maybe it was margarine. After she'd eaten two bricks, she stopped and looked at me with those beggar eyes. 'Keep eating!' I insisted to the whore. 'It's good for you! And once you've finished it all, the evidence will be gone and the Gestapo will have no reason to punish you!'

"My buddies were laughing. So as she stood there, hesitating, I ordered the Ukrainian pigs to force-feed her.

One held her arms. The other kept her mouth open with one hand and pushed the butter directly into her throat, brick by brick, until the whole thing was gone. She looked like a goose being fattened. I'll never forget it! We all laughed like crazy, and the Jewish whore howled, 'Oy, vay! Oy, vay!' "

"That's a good story," said a sergeant from Berlin, a house painter before the war. "But mine is even better. There was a bearded old Jew in the town of Brody who was impudent enough to cross in front of me. When I see a black cat or a Jew in a black coat, I shoot."

The diners roared with laughter. They liked the comparison between the cat and the Jew — both black and both hairy.

"So I ordered him to run. You know, for exercise. As he was running, I shot him in one leg. The dirty thing started hopping on his good leg and quacked, just like your Jewess, 'Oy, vay!' So to keep him in balance, I shot him in the other leg. That bastard, he stopped hopping! He lay on the cobblestones and kept quacking. It wasn't fun any longer, so I left him there for the SS to finish off."

Day after day, the stories followed one another and they all laughed, slapped each other on the back and clapped their hands on their knees.

Rarely would I hear a German lament the atrocities in human terms. There was one, a man in his early fifties. He came from Saarbrücken, had a French accent and pitied the Russians and the Jews. But he did it in private, where only I might hear. He must have felt that I was more sensitive than the others — or who knows? Maybe he, too, was a Jew disguised as a German.

All my German companions shared one fear: what would happen to them if they fell into the hands of the Russians. Each of them had the same dream, to serve on the western front. There, sooner or later, they would become British, or even better, American prisoners of war. They had fewer and fewer illusions about the success of Hitler's Blitzkrieg.

While discharging my daily chores I would carry on with my own little acts of sabotage. So far, no one understood what I was doing. The winter was a severe one, so cold that a piece of butter if left outside for a short while would become as hard as stone.

My crews were not repairing the roads with butter but with my formula of sand and lime. In winter it would get to be as hard as stone but — come spring, it would turn the roads to mud. I felt that I was ordering my own brand of tank traps to be built, to help the German war machine on its way to destruction.

I prayed to the God of Israel to take me far from there when the thaw came, lest the first wall in sight become my grave stone.

Abo, now officially the chaplain's helper, visited me a couple of times. We shared news about the front, and planned our final moves. Both of us wanted to go back to Dolginzewo, where father and Wilo were still waiting — we hoped.

One day we parted with a promise to each other. If we survived and were liberated, we'd make our way to Dnepropetrovsk. By now, the area around Novyj Bug was a battle zone. To step out of the relative safety of the unit might be considered an act of foolishness. But for me, it was only the response to an urgent drive. Dolginzewo meant father, Wilo and, maybe, Abo. I had no choice but to leave my present shelter.

A few weeks later, I stepped into the lieutenant's office.

I greeted him with the obligatory "Heil Hitler," and said I had a favor to ask. He was friendly, but I could see that he was unusually tense. The latest news was disturbing.

I started. "You'll laugh at me. It seems ludicrous even to me when I think about it. But I must do it."

"Must do what?"

"I have to go to Dolginzewo, to retrieve some things there."

He looked at me as though I was crazy.

"To Dolginzewo? With what's happening all around us? For a few rags?"

"That's just it. It's not for the clothing."

"What is it, then? Have you hidden gold there?" He glanced at me sharply.

"No gold. It's more than that. I left a sacred medallion that belonged to my German great-grandmother. And an antique vase, hers too, in which I hid the medallion. Those are family treasures. I must get them back."

The lieutenant was a sensible man.

"Although I'm reluctant to do it, I'll issue a travel permit that will allow you to move within the front lines. I must say that I admire your guts. With all those partisans and saboteurs around, you're running a great risk. Not to mention that you might even be killed by friendly fire."

I knew all that, but I wanted to be with my family when the moment of liberation came, and I was sure that it would be soon.

The next morning, immediately after roll call, I picked up my permit and an additional ration book. The lieutenant had granted me a ten day furlough. I hoped that during the period of my leave the Red Army would cross the line at the Dneper River.

I left my blankets as well as some clothing with my Ukrainian hosts, packed a knapsack and had breakfast in the mess hall. "God," I prayed silently over the scrambled eggs and grits, "let this be my last German meal!" Then, boarding one of the unit's trucks, I rode to a transfer point. After an hour's wait, I hitched a ride on a halftrack headed for Krivoi Rog.

It was dark when we arrived at the driver's base camp.

"I'd like to continue," I said to him — by now he had become at ease with me. "Could you help me get a ride on one of the local trucks?"

"Not at night," he said. "Only soldiers are allowed in the combat zone after curfew. I'll tell you what — have dinner with me in the commissary, then I'll get you a bed, and you'll be on your way tomorrow morning."

I had no option. My new friend put me in a tiny room next to the commissary, took me to breakfast in the morning and convinced a soldier who drove a munitions truck to let me ride next to him. Thus, the last leg of my trip was spent in the rear truck, in a convoy moving toward Dolginzewo. For several hours, I listened to an incessant stream of cursing; the driver chose to unload his frustrations on

Ukrainian peasants, dogs, Jews and potholes. Finally we neared my destination.

"Thanks for the ride, Hans," I said. "I'll walk from here. I've only got a few kilometers to go." I needed that walk, to purge my ears of his profanities and to prepare myself for whatever lay ahead.

Dolginzewo had become a ghost town. Heavy clouds laden with snow hung over the area. I played a guessing game with myself as I walked. Father. Alive? Wilo. Still there? Lida. Will she remember me?

I stopped in front of the widowed sisters' house. My heart was racing. I hesitated, then knocked.

I heard an "Oh!" from one of the sisters. Then I heard, "It's he!" from Wilo. Then there was a gasp from father, who thought for a moment that I might be one of the remaining Wehrmacht soldiers, arriving for a final accounting. Then all was radiance and joy as they recognized me.

"And do you recognize me?" father asked, smiling. "I'm good old Mr. Tyszkiewicz. So, Mr. Nowak? How are things?"

"I have greetings for you." I threw my knapsack on the floor. "From a Mr. Piotr Siminski."

"Where is he? What is he doing?" father and Wilo asked simultaneously.

"He's all right. He works in a Wehrmacht field hospital. As a helper to the chaplain," I added casually. "Now, don't ask any more questions. It's a long story, which I'm sure will have a happy ending. I'll tell you about it when we eat."

I washed and we sat down to a repast of canned meat for Wilo and me and vegetable soup for father. Through the long years of Nazi domination, he had never quit following the strict law of kashruth.

I unfolded the story of my recent adventures and those of Abo too, bringing tears to father's eyes and prompting him to praise the Lord in heaven.

The account of father's and Wilo's life was simple: continuous hunger, cold and fright. It wasn't exciting, just heartbreaking.

Late in the morning, we parted. I still felt that the three of us should pretend to be mere friends. Besides, I wanted to say hello to Lida and move back into my old room.

As I stood in front of her door, blasts from heavy guns shook the ground. There were intermittent bursts of fire in the night sky. A battle was being fought close by.

"Who's there?" came a faint voice from inside. Lida was scared.

"It's I! Please open up, Lida! It's Nowak!"

She threw the door open, but then backed away in fear. She had never seen me in a German army uniform. It took her a few minutes to accept the new me.

"You've got to get rid of those," she said, pointing with disgust to the fatigues.

"I will. As soon as you take me to my room."

In no time, I was the old Stanislaw Nowak, the man in the brown leather jacket—my Wehrmacht garb burned to ashes in Lida's stove.

"Nobody should ever connect you with that uniform," she scolded. "If the Germans catch you in it, they'll shoot you as a deserter. The Russians would certainly shoot you."

She wasn't happy about my sleeping in my old room,

either. "You should stay in the underground hideout," she advised. "It's cramped, but it will be for only a couple of days, maybe for only a few hours."

"Let me sleep in my bed," I pleaded. "One night. I'll move into the hole first thing in the morning."

That was what I did. At dawn, I moved into the pit that we had dug some time before. From there, hidden under a considerably diminished pile of potatoes, I heard the last, desperate convulsions of the Nazi army. Sometimes, I heard the rapid thump of men's boots; that would be a company of soldiers in hasty retreat. On other occasions, the noise of crisp marching would reach me in my den; that would be a rear patrol, probably the Waffen SS. Trucks drove incessantly along the main street of the town, heading west. Finally, the search-and-destroy — Sonderkommandos — mines blowing up the track beds and rails.

Now and then a group of soldiers would break into the house, curse Lida, accuse her of hiding partisans and demand vodka before leaving. On the fourth day, the last group of German soldiers invaded her house. They were unshaven, dirty and defeated. All they asked for was a minute by the fire, a glass of water and a slice of bread. Those were the last pitiful shreds of Hitler's mighty armed forces that we were to see.

The days dragged. Cringing in my grave-like hideout for one long week, I counted the hours and minutes. I had the sensation of living in the midst of a never ending earthquake. Artillery shells burst all around us, tanks fought bloody battles, and from time to time a plane dropped a bomb for good measure.

At last came February 21, 1944! The tremors suddenly stopped. The silence that followed was so deep that it hurt my ears worse than had the noise of explosions. The quiet was threatening. I had lived through years of screaming, shouting, shooting, crying and moaning, but I couldn't stand that blessed stillness.

The calm lasted almost the entire morning. Then guns burst all around in rapid fire. I heard the clop of boots near my hideout. A frightened man implored in German, "Kamerad! Schiessen Sie nicht! Hitler ist kaputt! Don't shoot comrade! Hitler's done for!" "Yob twoyu matj, ty preklatyj Niemietz!" was the curt reply. "You bastard, you damned German!" Then more rattle from an automatic gun. Someone kicked Lida's door open and asked if all was well inside.

"Our boys!" she exclaimed. "We've waited for you three long years! God bless you!"

I felt like a groundhog brought out from hibernation by its zookeeper when Lida and her aunt uncovered my burrow. Like caviar, freedom is precious, but a person must train his palate for it. For some time, I stayed in my hole, a prisoner of liberty. Finally, prompted by Lida's joyous shouts, I left my lair and stepped out of the house. In front of the door lay a dead German officer. Russian soldiers had stripped him of anything useful, just as the war had stripped them of the respect they had once felt for the dead. In their haste to remove the officer's clothes they had broken his neck — the symbol of the end.

I walked toward the widows' house. The main street, until then empty and forbidding, was filling with Russian soldiers, happy women and civilians who had sprung out from nowhere. Jeeps, trucks and troop carriers covered with dirty white camouflage sheets pressed westward.

Father and Wilo stood in front of the widows' house. Father embraced me and tearfully recited a Jews' holiest prayer, "Shmah Yisroel. Adonia Eolheynu. Adonai ehad!" It is formal acknowledgement that the God of Israel, God our Lord, is the one God.

All three of us were crying and kissing openly in front of the crowd passing by. No one could imagine that we were three Polish Jews, a father and two sons, survivors of a horror difficult to describe.

For us the war was over.

|||| |||| |||| |||| |||| ||||

CHAPTER

13

An End to Disguises

T HE EUPHORIA of the first two days ended with the
arrival of the Soviet State Security Police — the NKVD, as
it was called before it became the KGB. These weren't the
simple soldiers we'd seen before, living today or perishing
by the bullet tomorrow. They were hardened men, raised
on distrust and unimpressed by death — highly skilled in
torture. Early in 1940, when they had begun to suspect
that there might be a few spies in the sea of Polish refugees
in Russia, they had ordered the entire refugee population
deported to the Siberian forest. The NKVD did not worry
about the human cost of its activities.

Now began one-on-one interviews with every remaining inhabitant of Dolginzewo.

I was a stranger, I was healthy, I was of an age when I should be in the army. But what mostly aroused suspicion was that I was a Pole who had been chief engineer for a German contractor. Therefore, I was one of the first to be summoned to the NKVD field headquarters, a temporary office established in what had been the Wening barracks.

I sat in a room where I had trembled before on numerous occasions during Wening's staff meetings, surrounded by Germans, fearful of being unmasked and hoping that the Red Army would retake the place and set me free.

"What is your name?" my interrogator began.

"Stanislaw Nowak. In reality, Uri Lichter. Also called Izio, Izio Lichter."

He looked at me with suspicion. "What are all those names? A bigos!" Bigos was an ancient Slavic dish, an assortment of meats cooked with cabbage or sauerkraut. I had no simple answer. How should I explain all this to an NKVD man? A well-known anecdote from the days of Soviet occupation of Lvov, in 1939, came to mind. The Russians were issuing the passports, or identity cards, to inhabitants deemed safe enough to continue living in the city. A manicurist, the story went, had applied for a passport.

"What is your occupation?" the policeman at the desk asked her. "I'm a manicurist," was the answer. The Soviet Union was, at that time, a very unsophisticated country, and the man asked what a manicurist was.

"I work in a barbershop. Men visit me and I soak their hands in warm water, then I clean their nails and cut them. It makes them feel good."

The policeman turned to his supervisor, who had been listening intently to this job description. "Comrade supervisor! I heard the woman talk, but I still don't know what she does for a living." The supervisor mused for a minute. Then, with the light of understanding in his eyes, he said simply, "Pishy prosto 'Bladj!' Just put down, 'hooker!' "

I knew that my explanation would be complicated. I told the man my story, including all about Abo, mother, father and Wilo.

He nodded attentively as I spoke. When I finished, he had his mind made up.

"Then, you're nothing but a spy!"

I was shocked. "A Ukrainian collaborator," my inquisitor added. "You will be hanged if you don't tell me the whole truth."

"But I told you the *truth!* I'm a Jew!" I was panic-stricken.

"You are a Nazi spy," he insisted. "Otherwise, what would you be doing in Dolginzewo, where Hitler had his war machine working until just recently? I'll give you another night to think things over. If you don't change your story, you'll hang like the other spies out there."

"I haven't done anything wrong!" I pleaded. After all I had lived through, after outwitting the SS, the Gestapo, the Vlasov bandits and the Ukrainian police, I was to be hanged by friendly hands.

I was interrogated again and again, always in the

middle of the night. The questions were always the same — repeat all the names, places and dates in your story — so that they could check their accuracy. The interrogators' conclusion was always the same: "You are a spy, and we will hang you."

Once more, fate, or was it God, intervened. On the morning of the third day, the special unit of the NKVD that had been questioning me, called the Osobo-Otdiel, moved west and was replaced by another contingent. I was brought upstairs to a captain of the regular security police. As he interrogated me, he showed a knowledge of Yiddish, and it seemed a possibility that he was also Jewish.

The captain listened to my story at length, interrupting me only occasionally as though testing my skill in Yiddish. Indeed, his first order aimed at having me prove my Jewishness was, "Say something in Yiddish!" When I asked what he wanted me to say, he answered, "Say: 'kiss my ass.' " After I had delivered the appropriate translation, he seemed to feel more at ease with me.

This hardened officer seemed to show some emotion as he listened to my account of Nazi atrocities, and after some deliberation, he let me go — free.

"You're lucky," he said, "that the special unit left in such a hurry. They would have hanged you. Well, I can't give you any papers in your original name. All I can do is advise you to leave Dolginzewo immediately. Take your father and your little brother. Go to Dnepropetrovsk. Maybe something can be done for you there."

It is almost impossible to describe the elation that father, Wilo and I felt at the moment of our second liberation. The following morning, we left the Ukrainian town where so much had happened to us and which had contributed so much to our survival.

Before leaving, I went to see Lida one last time. She was worried because I had been arrested and held for almost three days. I told her that it was dangerous for me to stay any longer in Dolginzewo, and that I had to find my family in Poland. I didn't burden her with the details of my real background. We parted without my giving her my real name or telling her that I was a Jew.

We traveled in a freight train, seated on top of a shipment of coal, and reached Dnepropetrovsk at night. The first thing that happened to us, as we left the railroad station, was our arrest by a Russian MP patrol.

The very documents that we had cherished so dearly, the papers covered with German signatures and the rubber stamps with the swastika, now worked against us. The three of us were thrown in jail.

That night was like my first arrest. I could see the heartless NKVD interrogator and hear him say, "You'll be hanged!" I also remembered the SS, particularly Obersturmbannführer Grzymek, who with his finger assigned life or death in the Judenlager of Lvov. To the west, the Gestapo was vanishing quickly; here, the shadow of the NKVD was rising, and I, a minor player who owed his and his family's survival to his wits alone, was caught between one and the other in a senseless game of politics.

The new scene was a familiar one. We were back in a filthy cell populated by unkempt men of all ages and backgrounds. Only this time, instead of being called partisans, it was collaborators.

In the morning, two guards brought us before a judge

for interrogation and sentencing. The judge, a young man, sat at his desk on a podium. As our fake Polish names were called, we stood up and faced him. When the preliminaries were over, the judge spoke to "Mr. Tyszkiewicz."

I intervened. "This is my father. He doesn't speak Russian or Polish. He's a Jew. He speaks only Yiddish. And his name isn't Tyszkiewicz. He is Yossel Lichter. I am Uri Lichter. And this is my brother Wilo. We are neither Germans nor Poles, we are Jews in hiding."

"Where are you from?" the judge asked father in *Yiddish*.

"We are from Lvov," father answered. "I am a Jew."

"And your name is Lichter?" I could detect some slight emotion in the judge's voice. "Tell me please, reb Yossel, were you a Furweser, one of the officials in the Shul Hadushim?"

"Yes!" father said. "How did you know that?"

"My own father worshiped in that shul. I had my bar mitzvah there," the judge said, then stopped to regain his composure. "Maybe you know what happened to *my* parents and sister?" He gave us his name. "My entire family remained in Lvov."

We had no news for him. All we had was the sensation that a miracle was happening. It was on that rare occasion when our Jewish past saved us, rather than condemned us. We were released and the judge ordered the local police to give us proper identification documents. He also told us that there were a few other survivors from Lvov now living in Dnepropetrovsk. This was my third and final liberation.

We were now free but we were also desperate. My

father, Wilo, and I found ourselves in a strange city with no place to live. As we wandered around looking, we were reminded of the judge's final remarks. He had informed us about other survivors from Lvov and their location in the city. The judge's advice saved us.

At one particular location we found a middle aged couple from Lvov who had survived — liberated several months before. They had found a tiny apartment, which they offered to share with us. Now at least we were able to look for our own lodging and live with some comfort.

Of the three of us I was the only one able to work. Father was spent, both emotionally and physically, and Wilo, now fourteen, was seriously undernourished. We were virtually starved and food was only available with the presentation of government issued coupons. I had to find a job and obtain ration books.

After several days I found a job as an office employee in a government supply cooperative. The pay was minimal; however, I was allowed to sleep in the large office, and also have my father and Wilo stay with me. The three of us would sleep in the office either on the bare floor or on an office desk. We no longer had to impose on the couple from Lvov.

My salary barely covered our food needs, and we had no personal effects left which could be exchanged for food. Yet we continued with some hope. We knew that the war on the Eastern front was still raging. At least we had distanced ourselves from that horror. Most trying for the three of us was our loneliness, and the fact that we missed Abo, our sisters, and our mother.

A month later at the end of March another miracle happened. Abo arrived in Dnepropetrovsk and found us. After an emotional reunion we settled down and pieced together our individual stories. Father, Wilo and I described the events that brought us to Dnepropetrovsk. Abo then recounted his stay in the military hospital and subsequent adventures leading to his liberation. This was his story.

He had continued working with the hospital chaplain for a short period of time, and was later transferred to the hospital supply department. At the beginning of March, 1944, with the Russian army advancing, the hospital was ordered to evacuate. All personnel were expected to move westward.

Finally in the ensuing chaos Abo saw his opportunity to slip away. During the evacuation he left the fleeing Germans and found a Russian family which was willing to give him sanctuary until the advancing Russian columns arrived.

Abo, however, was not yet home free. In his elation, he greeted the Russian soldiers and happily announced that he was actually a Polish Jew, and that the German identification papers he carried had been falsified. Wartime, however, breeds suspicion, and the Russians were not satisfied with his story. Abo became a prisoner. The Russians arrested him as a suspected spy.

NKVD officers interrogated and threatened him for an entire week, demanding that he sign a confession. Abo refused, insisting that he was a Jew. He had suffered enough at the hands of the Germans; now to confess that he was a Nazi collaborator was unthinkable.

His luck changed, when it turned out that one of the NKVD interrogators was Jewish. After lengthy questioning he convinced his Russian captor that he was indeed Jewish. Finally Abo was truly free — now to find and be reunited with his father and brothers. His destination was Dnepropetrovsk where he hoped we were alive and well.

He reached Dnepropetrovsk at the end of March, 1944. First, he went to the city market to inquire about Polish citizens, which, at that time, usually meant Polish Jews. By luck he met a Polish shoemaker. He and his wife were Jews. They knew where the Lichter family was staying and they brought Abo to us.

With Abo's safe return we were confronted with a new problem. Now that we were four, my office management would not allow us all to sleep in the office. It was now imperative that I find a place immediately, for my father and brothers. A friend in the office told me about a dilapidated shack that was unoccupied and available. It was located several streets down from the office where I worked.

The condition of the shack was deplorable, but at least it provided a roof over their heads. There were no furnishings, no kitchen facilities, and no heating. At night to ward off the cold Russian nights they slept huddled together on the floor fully dressed, covered with one blanket, with father sleeping between Wilo and Abo.

The director of the government office who had hired me was soon transferred. A new director arrived from Siberia with his family, and he moved into several empty rooms located above the office. He was a Russian Jew, who had managed to save his family by fleeing from Dnepropetrovsk to Siberia for the duration of the Nazi occupation. He took a liking to me and moved me to a tiny room, in which the one bed filled the whole space.

On one occasion the director invited me to a family dinner. There I met my future wife, Fenia. She was the director's niece. She, together with her uncle and family, were the first ones to hear how I had survived the war.

Fenia was a medical student. Ours was love at first sight. After going together for a short while, we decided to get married, and a whole new life opened up in front of us.

Father and my brothers could not make a go of it, however, even with my financial support. Hearing that conditions in the Transylvanian town of Balta were somewhat better, they moved there, and settled down in what had been a Jewish ghetto created by the Rumanian fascist government. They stayed in Balta until September 1944.

Before leaving Dnepropetrovsk, to my great surprise, I met Wala, the Russian Jewish woman from Dolginzewo, the one to whom I had sent Wilo to warn her to flee.

Ever since the Red Army had liberated the southern Ukraine, she had been trying to find the person responsible for her and her daughter's survival. Her only clue was that a Polish boy named Stasio had brought her the word. In Dolginzewo, she was told that the Poles who had worked for Wening had gone to Dnepropetrovsk. So she traveled there, and by good fortune ran into me. She asked, "Do you remember that Polish boy, Stasio? Can you tell me where I can find him?"

"I know why you're asking about Stasio," I interrupted. "You need search no farther. I'll tell you the whole story. It will come as quite a surprise!"

She waited expectantly.

"Stasio," I began slowly, "is my youngest brother. I was the one who sent him to you. I saw the Gestapo order for your arrest. It described you as a Jewess, and asked Wening to turn you over to the SS." As Wala listened in amazement, I added the final flourish. "Stasio and I are Jewish. So is Piotr Siminski. We're all brothers."

She sobbed and tried to kiss my hand. "How can I repay you for what you've done?" she asked.

There was no need to repay us. She and I were links in a chain of people — kept alive by helping each other. I had saved Wala. Rozia had been saved by the Prachtels. There were good people in the world; one just had to look around to find them. There might not have been ten righteous people in Sodom and Gomorrah, but there were certainly many in Europe, even during the Holocaust when their own lives were at risk.

I held Wala, and let her cry on my shoulder.

Six weeks after Lvov was liberated, I returned there, using special travel permits obtained for me by my boss.

During my trip back to Lvov I experienced another one of the ironies of these unstable times. I was traveling on a train filled mostly with military personnel. For no apparent reason, our train was stopped near Shepetovka, in a barren region which was near the old Polish, Russian border. A Soviet military patrol surrounded the train and military police were dispatched to the individual cars.

One soldier entered my car and ordered all passengers to produce their identification. This meant that we had to show him our passports and travel permits. As he stood giving orders he presented an almost comical picture. He was a short stocky Russian. He held a submachine gun which looked almost too long for him to handle. He finally reached my seat and picked up my papers. He first stared at me and then at my papers. Then he held my identification papers up to the light turning them and looking through the paper. Without warning he started yelling. "These papers are falsified. The stamps on these papers were forged. They were made with the use of potato stamps."

His outburst had a strange effect on me. My thoughts raced back to a time less than a year before, when I had traveled with truly forged identification papers, and those documents had contained forged stamps fashioned from potatoes. As the corporal continued yelling I thought of the numerous times that my forged documents had been scrutinized by the Nazis, and how those Nazis known for their exactness and detail had accepted them without question. Those phony papers had saved my life on several occasions. Now, when I had legitimate documentation I was being accused of traveling with forged papers.

My emotions betrayed me and I started to laugh. The more I laughed the madder the short corporal became. He was now furious and yelled at me. "Why are you laughing you idiot? You better know that here I am the authority. I am the general here."

With his submachine gun aimed directly at me, he

ordered me to step off the train, and we marched outside toward a small hut. There his commanding officer had set up temporary headquarters.

Inside the hut, as I stood by perplexed, the corporal explained to his officer that he had discovered that I was carrying falsified documents. The officer took over. He gave the appearance of rank, and calmly reviewed my traveling papers. Fortunately for me he didn't agree with his corporal. He accepted my papers as genuine and curtly dismissed me. I was now free again to continue my journey to Lvov.

I found the town in a shambles. Like litter on a street, the few ragged survivors could be seen, here seated in a doorway, there hunched against a wall, or roaming aimlessly or staring with unseeing eyes at faces they did not recognize. Most of those survivors stayed in and around the Synagogue Hadushim. This had become a gathering place for them. They were no more than a few hundred, including those from the small cities and villages around Lvov.

My first concern was to find Rozia, my mother, and my older sister Riwka, taken from us in 1941. When I inquired about Riwka my worst fears were confirmed. She had been picked up at her workplace with many other women. They had been placed on the first transports from Lvov and had been gassed in Belzec by the Nazis.

Rozia was alive and well. She had blossomed into a beautiful young lady. Mrs. Prachtel and her daughter had taken good care of her, even though shielding a Jew could have cost them their lives.

When I asked her to join us, she broke into tears.

"This is my family," she pleaded with me. "I love these people. It is thanks to them that I'm alive today. Please, don't take me away from here!"

It was a shock for me. I understood my sister's feelings, but I could not accept them. Mrs. Prachtel proved helpful. A mature and wise woman, she sympathized with the child. She knew how to speak to her, and tried to persuade her that she belonged with us. Later, when father, Abo and Wilo came to Lvov from Balta and reclaimed the family residence, it was somewhat easier to convince Rozia that, without her, the family would not be the same. She became a Lichter again.

But we could not find mother. All we succeeded in getting were unconnected bits of information. We heard that the day before the final liquidation of the Judenlager, the Prachtels' daughter had gone to see mother at Ryzewski's company kitchen and offered her shelter. Mother declined the hospitality of these "righteous Poles," not wanting to jeopardize their lives.

One of our former Polish customers, Mrs. Swirski, told us that on the day of the final liquidation, mother had escaped from a burning building that had been surrounded by SS and the police. Dodging bullets, she arrived at the Swirski house, and had spent the night hiding in their bathtub.

In the morning, disguised as a Ukrainian peasant, she left the Swirskis and headed for the city limits. There she had an appointment with a guide who had promised to smuggle her into Rumania. That was the last time she was ever seen.

For the next three years we searched for her. We crisscrossed Europe. We read every name in the logs of survivors. We left pleas of love and despair. We hoped that someone might know her and give her our message.

Our search was to no avail. She had come to this life blessed by the Almighty — to give us life and joy, yet at the end, she would leave all alone to join the invisible spirit of God.

The several months that we remained in Lvov were difficult for us. The once friendly and familiar streets and houses now reflected only shadows of the dead — constant reminders of the horrors that had taken place there. For us, Lvov was a nightmare of the past.

The family decided to leave and to journey toward western Europe. We stopped for a time in Krakow. There, we experienced a Polish population still hostile toward Jews. The Poles showed no remorse.

During our short stay in Krakow the local Poles began agitating against Jews and planned a pogrom against the few survivors. It was only by the efforts of the new Polish peoples police, created and supervised by the Russian authorities, that another bloodbath was averted.

Because of these awful facts we left Krakow and entered Austria. From Vienna a relief agency helped transport us to Germany where we were placed in a refugee camp called the Einring. This camp was full of Jewish survivors from all the east European countries. The awful conditions in the camp forced me to increase my efforts to find us more normal living conditions elsewhere.

I learned that a prewar friend from Lvov had survived, and was now in a city near Nürenberg called Furth. After finding and meeting him, I returned to the refugee camp and moved the family to Furth — for the first time in years, I felt relief from constantly being on the run.

We started to resume our respective formal educations. Father returned to his Talmudic studies, and joined the renowned Rabbi Shapiro from Warsaw, himself a survivor from a concentration camp.

A rabbinical court was created in Furth, and my father was selected to be the head of this court. This very honorable position was given to him because of his great Talmudic knowledge. He was again referred to as Reb Yosef.

After living for almost two years in Furth, father and Rabbi Shapiro advised the family to say Kaddish, the prayer for the dead, for mother. God rest her soul. An arbitrary but fitting date was declared for her death, the holy day of Yom Kippur, 5704, or 1943 of the world calendar.

⫟⫟ ⫟⫟ ⫟⫟ ⫟⫟ ⫟⫟ ⫟⫟

CHAPTER

14

Postlude:

Settling an Account

B EFORE BECOMING fully involved in my new life, I had a
promise to keep. One I had made to myself a long time
before.

In the spring of 1947, with two friends I went to the
building in Zürndorf, Germany, where the offices of the
Wening Construction Company were housed.

"I'd like to see Herr Wening," I said to a heavy,
middle-aged woman who opened the door. "It is regarding
a very personal matter."

Herr Wening, once a Nazi Party member and a rich
contractor in the occupied southern Ukraine, was now a
peaceful German businessman.

As we entered his simple office, he looked closely at us. A spark of recognition flickered in his eyes as he looked more closely at me. He clasped his head with his two hands, and exclaimed with fake joy, "Ach du lieber! Herr Nowak! Of course."

Then, recovering his poise, he said in his most correct German, "Please, gentlemen! Please, do sit down!"

I grinnned, as my companions and I took seats.

"Yes, Herr Wening! No one else but me!"

"Dear God! I thought so often about you! I'd say to myself, 'Who knows what happened to my friend Nowak? What might those Bolsheviks have done to him?' "

"Well, I am here, Herr Wening. And I have a surprise for *you!*"

"Where do you live? How are you? Tell me all about yourself!"

By his questions he sought to veil growing anxiety.

"I live in Nüremberg now, Herr Wening — and about the surprise . . ." I continued dryly. "My name is *not* Stanislaw Nowak. I am Uri Lichter."

"Well . . ." Something began to penetrate.

"These two men are survivors, they live in a refugee camp now. They are my friends."

Wening's face became pale, and as in the old days, when under stress, he sweated profusely.

"Do you remember Wala? The Jewess who disappeared when you were ordered to turn her in to the Gestapo?"

Wening's lips opened in an almost inaudible, "Yes. Her disappearance caused me a lot of trouble."

"Well, I was the person who tipped her off. I sent her the message through the Polish boy Stasio, and *he* was my brother Wilo." I savored the situation.

"The other Pole — Piotr Siminski — my brother Abo, and, incidentally, I am, like these two men," I waved toward them, "a Jew!"

From pale grey, Wening's complexion turned to purple. He looked like a man who had just been struck by lightning. His lips moved, but not one more word came out. He leaned heavily on his desk.

Unrelenting, I added, "And for your work in the Ukraine, the Russian authorities are looking for you!"

Wening lost his composure. Prostrate in his chair, having difficulty catching his breath, he was a picture of dread and confusion. It was clear that his fear of the Russians was overwhelming. He whispered, "Is there anything I can do for you, Nowak? Anything?"

All three of us stood up at once. I replied, as coldly as I could, "Nothing, Herr Wening! Absolutely nothing!"

Thus having kept my promise to myself, I walked away, leaving behind much of my painful past. A simple act, perhaps, but one of great catharsis for me.

The family remained in Furth for about five years, until in 1951 when we received our entry visas and were able to move on, to the United States.

Though life improved for all of us, the experiences in the Judenlager of Lvov and those in the Ukraine are never to be forgotten. Those memories, though muted somewhat by time, are forever a part of us. It was our destiny to survive; we merely helped that destiny along a little.

THE LICHTER FAMILY TODAY

JOSEF LICHTER (ALIAS WLADYSLAW TYSZKIEWICZ):

After the liberation, Josef Lichter returned to the full practice of his religion. Eventually, he settled in Brooklyn, New York. From there, to his great joy, he was to see the rebirth and growth of his family, all of whose members continued to follow the strict rules of the Jewish faith. In 1965, before he died, his lifelong dream was fulfilled when he flew to Israel to meet his religious leader, the Hasidic, Belzer, Rabbi.

URI (IRE) LICHTER (ALIAS STANISLAW NOWAK):

Has pursued a career in architectural design and real-estate development in Miami. He and his wife have found great joy in their two sons and six grandchildren.

ABRAHAM (ABO) LICHTER (ALIAS PIOTR SIMINSKI):

Abo received a degree in structural engineering while still in Europe. He and his wife and three children first lived in New York City, then moved to Miami, where he is a professional engineer.

WOLF (WILO) LICHTER (ALIAS STASIO GRABOWSKI):

Wilo lives in Miami. His family consists of four children and two grandchildren. He has a doctorate in microbiology and is a professor at The University of Miami. Most of his work is devoted to cancer research.

ROZIA LICHTER DAVIDOVITZ (ALIAS HALINA KORECKA)

Rozia is the proud mother of seven children and grandmother of seven grandchildren. She and her family first moved to Canada and finally settled in Brooklyn.

SOZI[CHERUNGSKASSE]

СУСПІЛЬНА ОБ[ЕЗПЕЧА УBEZPIECZALNIA SPOŁECZNA]

[L]E[M]B[E]R G   Konto Nr. 21.010 bei der Zentrobank Lemberg

Konto bei der Emissionsbank   Ч. конто в Центробанку у Львові 21.010

Конто в Емісійному Банку   Telefon

Konto w Banku Emisyjnym we   Nr. konta Centrobanku we Lwowie 21.010

Ruf — Tenjrон — Telefon
Nr. 10.90, 51, 92, -88 :-:

LEMBERG   12.VII.1942.
Kopernikussir, 4.

№ 435.P.Z.42.

B e s t ä t i g u n g .

Es wird hiermit bestätigt, dass I. N O W A K Stanislaus geboren
am 4.5.1916 in Stanyr und wohnhaft in Lemberg, als Kontroleur
[...]s k[...] der Sozialversicherungskasse in Lemberg tätig
ist.

Der Genannte ist berechtigt die Kontrolle der Rentenempfänger
wohnhaften im Distrikte Galizien durchführen.

Es wird gebeten ihnen Hilfe leisten zu wollen.—

Der Leiter:

The author's false identification document in German, July 12,
1942, establishing him as a Pole named Stanislaus Nowak.

Self portrait (left), in pencil, Uri Lichter after liberation, signed
March 28, 1945.   Photo, (right) Miami, 1986.

Uri Lichter and Fenia his wife, Furth, Germany, 1947.

Josef Lichter (left), father. Photo from his false identification, establishing him as Wladyslaw Tyszkiewicz, 1943. Eva (Chava) Lichter (right), mother, 1943, killed by the Nazis after the liquidation of the Judenlager in Lvov.

House where the Lichter family lived before the German occupation of Lvov, (left 1941, right 1978).

Josef Lichter,
New York, 1960

Official identification for Wladyslaw Tyszkiewicz (alias Josef Lichter), a registered resident of Dolginzewo, October 21, 1943.

Der Gebietskommissar
Dnjepropetrowsk

Nr. ....

Eisenbahnberechtigungsschein

Der/die _____ Piotr Siminski _____
                              Vor- und Zuname

Beruf _____

beschäftigt bei _____
reist im dienstlichen Auftrag – in dringendem Interesse .
der Dienststelle _____

in der Zeit vom _____ bis _____

von _____ nach _____

Dieser Eisenbahnberechtigungsschein hat nur in Verbindung mit dem
_____ Gültigkeit.die Eisenbahn

von _____ nach _____

einmalig – mehrmalig zu benutzen.

Dnjepropetrowsk, den _____ 1943

Der Gebiet Kommisar
Dnjepropetrowsk
....

Official permit, allowing Piotr Siminski (alias Abraham
Lichter) to pass from Dnepropetrovsk to Lvov and return.
Signed and sealed by the District Kommisar, May 19, 1943.

Durchlaßschein Nr. D/769/43

für

Generalgouvernement —

(Angabe des oder der Gebiete in roter Schrift)

Piotr Siminski, Elektriker

(Vorname, Familienname, Beruf)

aus Lemberg

(Ständiger Wohnort, Straße, Hausnummer)

ist berechtigt, unter Vorlage des Passes — Paßersatzes — Kinderausweises — der Kennkarte — des amtlichen Lichtbildausweises[1])

Nr. 25/43

ausgestellt von Wiener Bau.Ges. Un in der Zeit

vom 19. 5. 1943 bis zum 23. 5. 1943

einmal[1]) und zurück[1]) — **wiederholt**[1])

über die amtlich zugelassenen Übergangsstellen nach

— _Generalgouvernement_ —

(Angabe des oder der Gebiete in roter Schrift)

zu reisen. Dnjepropetrowsk, den 19. 5. 1943

Der Gebietskommissar

Dnjepropetrowsk

(Dienststelle)

(Unterschrift)

[1]) Nichtzutreffendes streichen.

A 88 (1. 41) Reichsbruckerei, Berlin   Din 476 A 6

Pass signed and sealed by Kommandant F. A. Eisenblath of Dnepropetrovsk, allowing the electrician Piotr Siminski, employed by the Wiener Bauunternehmung Gesellschast to travel from May 19, 1943 through June 23, 1943. The firm was ficticious, the document was authentic.

Abraham (Abo) Lichter (left 1941, center after liberation, Krakow 1945 and right Miami, 1986).

Bescheinigung

Wir bestätigen hiermit, dass das Ukrain. Gefolgschaftsmitglied.

Grabowskij Stanislaw.

seinen Pass bezw. Personalausweis in unserem Büro hinterlegt hat.

A.-N. 128.

B.-N.

Dolginzewo, d 10.8.1943 Leonh. Wening Bauunternehmung Dolginze... (Bez. Dniepropetrowsk-Süd) Ukraine ...

Dolginzewo

Grabowskiy, Stanislaus

Leonh. Wening Bauunternehmung Dolginzewo (Bez. Dniepropetrowsk-Süd) Ukraine ...

Eisenbahn-Neubauamt · Dolginzewo

Gültig bis 31.11.43.

Employee identity cards for Stasio Grabowski (alias Wolf, Wilo, Lichter), dated October 8, 1943 and November 30, 1943, stamped "official" by Leonh. Wening Bauunternehmung Dolginzewo, Ukraine.

Wolf Lichter, 1943

Wolf Lichter
Krakow, 1945

Doctor Wolf Lichter,
Miami, 1986.

Rozia Lichter (left) before the Nazi occupation, Lvov, 1941. As
Halina Korecka (right), living under protection of the Prachtel
family, Lvov, 1943–44.

Rozia Lichter Davidovits, Brooklyn, New York, 1986.

ЗОРЯ

Орган Днепропетровского Обкома и Горкома КП(б)У
и областного Совета депутатов трудящихся

Информационный бюллетень | **Вторник, 22 февраля 1944 г.**

...чая Красная Армия, героически борющаяся за честь, свободу и независимость нашего Отечества против немецко-фашистских захватчиков!

(Из призывов ЦК ВКП(б) к 26 годовщине Красной Армии).

Итоги месячного наступления войск Ленинградского и Волховского фронтов

Войска Ленинградского фронта в первой половине января месяца перешли с боями занятии против немецко-фашистских войск, державших в осаде город ЛЕНИНГРАД; одновременно войска Волховского фронта начали наступление на город Новгород.

Войска Ленинградского фронта, ударами из районов ПУЛКОВО и южнее ОРАНИЕНБАУМ, прорвали сильно укрепленную, глубоко эшелонированную долговременную оборону немцев к юго-западу от ЛЕНИНГРАДА. В то же время войска Волховского фронта, форсировав реку ВОЛХОВ и верховье озера ИЛЬМЕНЬ, также успешно прорвали сильно укрепленную долговременную оборону немцев севернее и южнее НОВГОРОДА.

Наши войска, широко применяя обходные маневры в сочетании с фронтальными ударами, в первые пять—шесть дней наступления овладели основными укрепленными опорными пунктами немецкой обороны городами КРАСНОЕ СЕЛО, РОПША, НОВГОРОД, гарнизоны которых были окружены и уничтожены. Под ударами наших войск потерпела крушение сильнейшая оборона немцев, которую они сами расценивали, как неприступный и непреодолимый „северный вал", как „стальное кольцо" блокады ЛЕНИНГРАДА.

Преследуя разбитые части немцев, наши войска в ходе непрерывного наступления последовательно выбили противника с ряда промежуточных укрепленных рубежей и на подступах к реке ЛУГА и подошли к этой реке, где немцы пытались остановить наше наступление на заблаговременно построенном сильном оборонительном рубеже. Однако, решительными и умелыми действиями наших войск река ЛУГА была форсирована, а немецкие позиции на этой реке были прорваны в районе города ЛУГА и обойдены с флангов южнее КИНГИСЕПП и БАТЕЦКАЯ.

В ходе наступления наши войска за месяц боев продвинулись вперед на 150—250 километров, очистили от противника побережье Финского залива до устья реки НАРВА и всю территорию восточнее реки НАРВА и ЧУДСКОГО ОЗЕРА, выйдя на линию СЕРЕДКА, СТРУГИ, КРАСНОЕ, ПЛЮССА, УТОРГОШ, ШИМСК. Нашими войсками освобождены города ПЕТЕРГОФ, УРИЦК, РОПША, КРАСНОЕ СЕЛО, ПУШКИН, ПАВ-

ЛОВСК, ГАТЧИНА, МГА, ТОСНО, КИНГИСЕПП, ГДОВ, ЛУГА, ЛЮБАНЬ, ЧУДОВО, НОВГОРОД, районные центры Ленинградской области ВОЛОСОВО, ОСЬМИНО, ЛЯДЫ, ПОЛНА, ПЛЮССА, ОРЕДЕЖ, БАТЕЦКАЯ, УТОРГОШ, ШИМСК и около 4000 других населенных пунктов.

Освобождена важнейшая железнодорожная магистраль, связывающая ЛЕНИНГРАД с МОСКВОЙ — ОКТЯБРЬСКАЯ железная дорога, а также освобождены железнодорожные линии ЛЕНИНГРАД—ВОЛОГДА, ЛЕНИНГРАД—МГА—РЫБИНСК, ЛЕНИНГРАД—НОВГОРОД, ЛЕНИНГРАД—БАТЕЦКАЯ, ЛЕНИНГРАД—ЛУГА, ЛЕНИНГРАД—ОРАНИЕНБАУМ—ВЕЙМАРН, ЛЕНИНГРАД—КИНГИСЕПП, ВЕЙМАРН—ГДОВ, ГАТЧИНА—ТОСНО.

За месяц боев нанесено тяжелое поражение основным силам 18 армии немцев в составе: 11, 21, 24, 58, 61, 121, 126, 170, 212, 215, 225, 227, 290 пехотных и 28 легко-пехотных, 1, 9, 10, 12 и 13 авиаполевых дивизий, полицейской дивизии СС, испанского легиона, танково-гренадерских дивизий СС „Нидерланды", „Нордланд", „Фельдхерхалле", а также 12 танковых дивизий. Разгромлена крупная артиллерийская группировка тяжелой артиллерии главного командования немецкой армии, обстреливавшая ЛЕНИНГРАД и имевшая на своем вооружении 320 орудий калибром от 150—406 мм.

УНИЧТОЖЕНО: самолетов—97, танков—275, орудий разного калибра—1962, в том числе орудий калибра от 150 до 406 мм.—102, минометов—229, пулеметов—3842, автомашин—4278, складов разных—460.

Противник потерял только убитыми свыше 90 тысяч солдат и офицеров.

Нашими войсками ЗАХВАЧЕНЫ следующие трофеи: танков—189, орудий разного калибра—1852, в том числе орудий калибра от 150 до 406 мм.—178, минометов—2543, пулеметов—4660, винтовок и автоматов—42.000, снарядов разного калибра—более 1.000.000, патронов—17.000.000, автомашин—2648, железнодорожных вагонов—615, складов с военным имуществом—353.

Взято в плен 7200 немецких солдат и офицеров.

СОВИНФОРМБЮРО.

ОТ СОВЕТСКОГО ИНФОРМБЮРО

Оперативная сводка за 21 февраля

В течение 21 февраля юго-западнее и южнее города ЛУГА наши войска с боями заняли несколько населенных пунктов и среди них СЕЛИЩЕ, ВОЦКАЯ, КИРИЛЛКОВО, КИЛОШИЦЫ, ВАШКОВО, ИВАНОВСКАЯ, ПОХОНЬ, ГОРОДИЩЕ.

Западнее, юго-западнее и южнее озера ИЛЬМЕНЬ наши войска продолжали развивать успешное наступление и овладели районными центрами Ленинградской области городом СОЛЬЦЫ, ВОЛОТ, ПОДДОРЬЕ, районным центром Калининской области городом ХОЛМ, а также с боями заняли более 100 других населенных пунктов, в том числе БОЛЬШОЙ УТОРГОШ, НИЗОВА, ОСТРОВА, ИГНАТОВА, ЛОПОТУХА, БОЛЬШОЕ и МАЛОЕ ЗАБОРОВЬЕ, СВИНОРД, ИЛОВЕНКА, УГОЩА, ЦИПИНО, ГУЩИХА, СУХАРЕВО и железнодорожные станции НИЗЫ, СОЛЬЦЫ, ВЕРЕЩИНО, ШЕЛОНЬ, ВОЛОТ.

На КРИВОРОЖСКОМ направлении наши войска, перейдя в наступление, сломили сопротивление про-

тивника и овладели узловой железнодорожной станцией ДОЛГИНЦЕВО, а также с боями заняли более 50 населенных пунктов, в том числе НОВО-ИВАНОВКА, БОЖЕДАРОВКА, ВЕЧЕРНИЙ КУТ, БОЖАНОВО, НОВО-УКРАИНКА, ПОЛТАВЦЫ, АННОВКА, ИВАНОВКА, НОВЫЙ КРИВОЙ РОГ и железнодорожные станции РОКОВАТАЯ, КОЛОМИЙЦЕВО, КАГАНОВИЧ, РАДУШНАЯ. Наши войска вплотную подошли к городу КРИВОЙ РОГ и завязали бои на окраинах города.

На других участках фронта — разведка, артиллерийско-минометная перестрелка и в ряде пунктов бои местного значения.

В течение 20 февраля наши войска на всех фронтах подбили и уничтожили 40 немецких танков. В воздушных боях и огнем зенитной артиллерии сбито 11 самолетов противника.

Ответ. редактор Р. ХОМЯКОВА.

Тираж 2659 | Адрес редакции: Днепропетровск, улица Серова (быв. Садовая) № 5. | БД 1104.

Russian Army front line bulletin of February 22, 1944,
reporting that on February 21, 1944, the city of Dolginzewo
had been liberated by the Red Army.

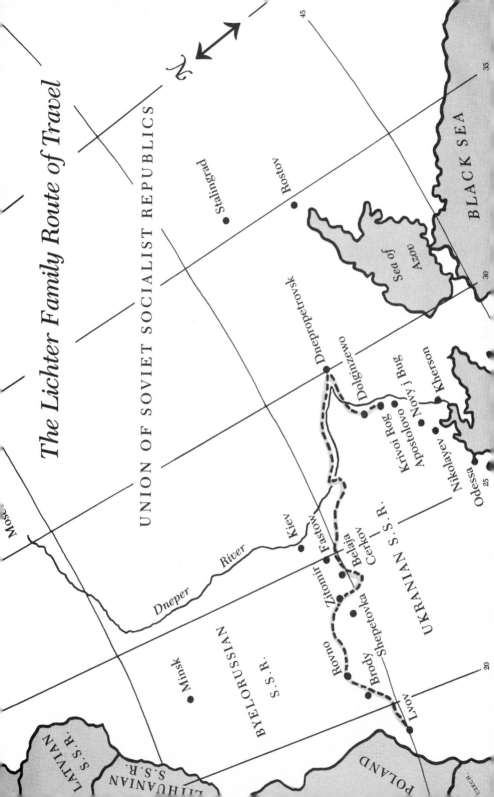

The Lichter Family Route of Travel

UNION OF SOVIET SOCIALIST REPUBLICS

Moscow

Stalingrad

Rostov

Sea of Azov

BLACK SEA

Dnepropetrovsk

Dolginzewo

Krivoi Rog

Apostolovo Nowy j Bug

Kherson

Nikolayev

Odessa

Dneper

River

Kiev

Fastow

Zitomir

Belaja Cerkov

Rovno

Shepetovka

Brody

Lvov

UKRANIAN S. S. R.

BYELORUSSIAN S. S. R.

Minsk

LATVIAN S.S.R.

LITHUANIAN S.S.R.

POLAND

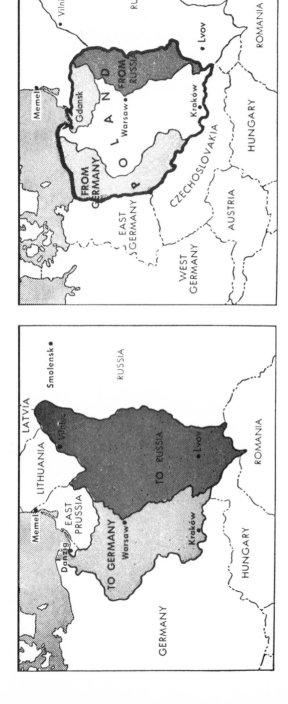

Russia and Germany split Poland in half, in 1939, before the second World War (left). After the war, Poland regained territory from Germany and from Russia. The current boundary, (right).

The Nazi plan for empire was to subjugate all of European
Russia up to the Urals. Their advance was halted in the winter
of 1942.

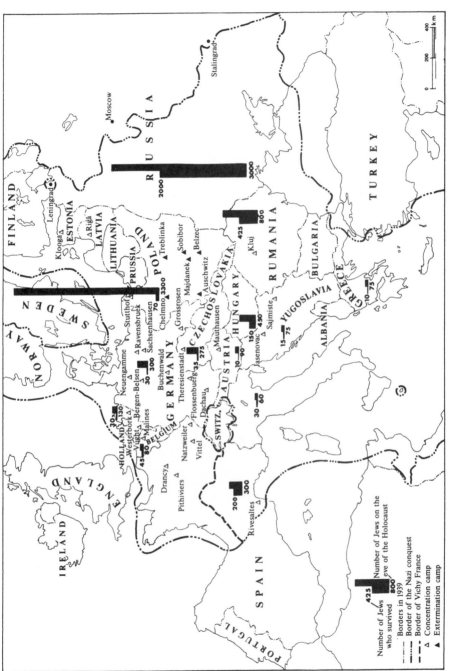

Concentration Camps and Death Camps where the "Six Million Jews" perished

War in Europe: Hitler's Calendar

1938

MARCH: Hitler forces Anschluss on Austria and declares it part of the German Reich.

SEPTEMBER OCTOBER: Germany occupies the Sudetenland, a part of Czechoslovakia, inhabited by ethnic Germans.

Great Britain accedes to the German demands in the infamous accord signed in Munich by Prime Minister Neville Chamberlain.

France, which had a mutual-defense treaty with Czechoslovakia, refuses to act without Great Britain.

German troops move into the Sudetenland on October 1.

NOVEMBER: German mobs, aided and abetted by Storm Troopers and Police, burn and destroy synagogues and smash Jewish businesses, in what came to be known as Kristallnacht, the Night of the Broken Glass. This was the worst pogrom until the systematic extermination of the Jews, "the final solution," began, three years later.

1939

MARCH: Hitler's troops march into Czechoslovakia. He proclaims it a German protectorate.

Chamberlain declares that Great Britain will support Poland if it attacked.

AUGUST: Germany and the Soviet Union sign a non-aggression pact, promising not to enter into any alliance against each other.

SEPTEMBER: Germany invades Poland on September 1, and on September 17, the Red Army invades Poland. Poland ceases to exist as the Soviet Union and Germany divide it between themselves. The city of Lvov becomes part of Russia.
Great Britain and France declare war on Germany.

1940

MAY: German troops invade France through Belgium, Holland and Luxembourg.

JUNE: France surrenders and signs an armistice with Germany.

AUGUST-
SEPTEMBER: The Battle of Britain.

OCTOBER: Hitler postpones a planned invasion of Great Britain.

1941

JUNE: Germany invades the Soviet Union along a two thousand mile front.

JULY: The Germans reach Kiev in the south and encircle Leningrad in the north.

AUGUST: Smolensk falls.

SEPTEMBER: The Germans push toward Moscow.

OCTOBER:	German progress is slowed.
DECEMBER:	Germany declares war on the United States after the Japanese attack on Pearl Harbor. The Soviets begin a counter attack against the German forces.

1942

JUNE:	The Germans begin a push toward Stalingrad.
NOVEMBER:	The Soviets counter attack, driving the Germans back.
DECEMBER:	Three hundred thousand Germans are surrounded at Stalingrad.

1943

JANUARY:	The German VI army, surrounded at Stalingrad, surrenders. The Soviet counter attack continues.
FEBRUARY:	Kursk, Rostov and Stalingrad are retaken by the Red Army.
JULY:	Allied forces invade Italy, and are stalled near Naples.
AUGUST:	Kharkov is retaken by the Soviets. The Germans fall back in the south to the Dneper.
SEPTEMBER:	In the north, Smolensk is retaken. The Russians cross the Dneper River south of Kiev. By the end of the month, the Russians reached Dnepropetovsk.

Russian forces are everywhere.
The Ukraine is liberated. The Russians are approaching Poland.

1944

FEBRUARY: Liberation of the Ukraine continues. Krivoi Rog falls to the Russians on February 22.

JUNE: The Russian spring offensive begins. It is aimed at Poland, Czechoslovakia and Germany.
Allied forces land in Normandy.

JULY: Lvov is liberated on July 27.

AUGUST: The Polish Home Army rises in rebellion in Warsaw but is crushed by the Germans.
Paris is liberated.
Allied forces land in southern France.

OCTOBER: The German counter offensive in the Battle of the Bulge, fails

FINIS, 1945

JANUARY: Russian troops reach Germany from the East.
Allied troops reach Germany from the West.

APRIL: Hitler commits suicide in his bunker in Berlin.

MAY: Germany surrenders.